CANADA

MAINE

Missouri River

MINNESOTA

DAKOTA
TERRITORY

WISCONSIN

MICHIGAN

Dresden

NEW YORK

VER.

N.H.

MASS.

CONN.   R.I.

Detroit

IOWA

Chicago

PENNSYLVANIA

New York

NEBRASKA   Omaha

Fremont
County

OHIO

INDIANA   Mercer
County

NEW JERSEY

Baltimore

Cincinnati

MD.   DELAWARE

Hamilton
County

Harpers Ferry   Washington, DC

ILLINOIS

Topeka

New Philadelphia

Abilene

St. Louis

WEST
VIRGINIA

Richmond

KANSAS   Lawrence

Ohio River

VIRGINIA

Dodge City

Wichita

MISSOURI

Lexington

KENTUCKY

Northampton
County

NORTH CAROLINA

Langston City

Hendersonville

Gallatin

Guthrie

Nashville

TENNESSEE

Oklahoma City

Pulaski

APPALACHIAN MTS.

OKLAHOMA
TERRITORY

ARKANSAS

SOUTH
CAROLINA

Red River

Atlanta

Mississippi River

Charleston

GEORGIA

TEXAS

MISSISSIPPI

ALABAMA

LOUISIANA   Meridian

Savannah

Shreveport

FLORIDA

ATLANTIC OCEAN

New Orleans

Rio Grande

Gulf of Mexico

0   200 miles

0   300 kilometers

N
W   E
S

The Geography
of Hope

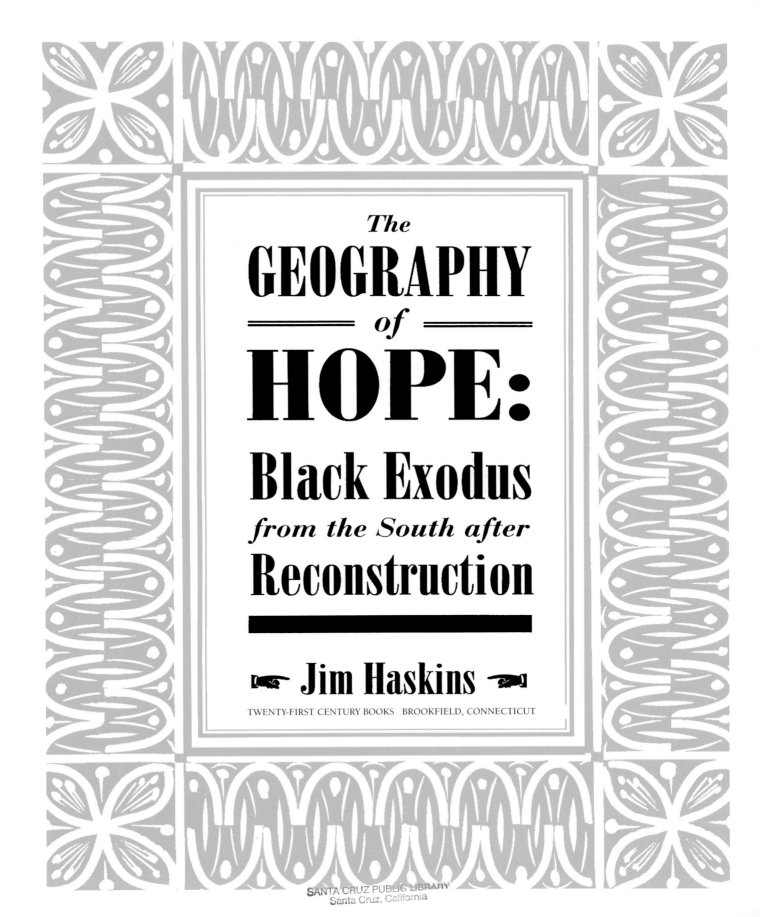

The
GEOGRAPHY
of
HOPE:
Black Exodus
from the South after
Reconstruction

Jim Haskins

TWENTY-FIRST CENTURY BOOKS   BROOKFIELD, CONNECTICUT

Chapter opening illustrations and design by Stephen Alcorn
© www.alcorngallery.com

Photographs courtesy of New York Public Library Picture Collection: p. 2; The Schomburg Center, New York Public Library: pp. 15, 44, 84; Corbis-Bettmann: p. 15 (bottom); North Wind Picture Archives: pp. 21, 26 (bottom), 43, 51, 53, 59, 67 (bottom), 92, 101, 104-105; Library of Congress: pp. 24, 37, 41 (top), 95; The Granger Collection, New York: pp. 26, 33 (both), 41 (bottom), 67 (top), 92-93; Kansas State Historical Society: pp. 38, 70-71, 77 (top), 114 (top); Western History Collections, University of Oklahoma Libraries: p. 77 (bottom); Dr. Barbara Richardson Collection: p. 114 (bottom); Archives & Manuscripts Division of the Oklahoma Historical Society: p. 123.

Library of Congress Cataloging-in-Publication Data
Haskins, James, 1941–
The geography of hope : Black exodus from the South after Reconstruction / Jim Haskins.
p. cm.
Includes bibliographical references (p.) and index.
Summary: Discusses the conditions of African Americans in the South before, during, and after the Civil War, and the migration of many former slaves, led by such men as Benjamin Singleton and Henry Adams, to the West looking for a better life.
ISBN 0-7613-0323-5 (lib. bdg.)
1. Afro-Americans—Southern States—Migrations—History—19th century—Juvenile literature. 2. Afro-Americans—West (U.S.)—History—19th century—Juvenile literature. 3. Afro-Americans—History—1863–1877—Juvenile literature. 4. Migration, Internal—United States—History—19th century—Juvenile literature. 5. Reconstruction—Juvenile literature. 6. Southern States—Race relations—Juvenile literature. [1. Afro-Americans—Southern States—History—19th century. 2. Afro-Americans—West (U.S.)—History—19th century. 3. Southern State—Race relations. 4. Reconstruction.] I. Title.
E185.2.H35 1999
973'0496073—dc21 98-33266 CIP AC

Published by Twenty-First Century Books
A Division of The Millbrook Press, Inc.
2 Old New Milford Road
Brookfield, Connecticut 06804
Visit us at http://www.millbrookpress.com

5 4 3 2 1

To Margaret Emily

Acknowledgments
I am grateful to Kathy Benson and Patricia A. Allen
for their help.

Contents

CHAPTER 1
Black Exodus
11

CHAPTER 2
The Peculiar Institution
17

CHAPTER 3
Reconstruction—
Presidential and Congressional
29

CHAPTER 4
Reconstruction Ends
47

CHAPTER 5
To Find a Place to Live Free
55

CHAPTER 6

Kansas: The Promised Land
61

CHAPTER 7

The "Singleton Colonies"
79

CHAPTER 8

The Exodusters of 1879
87

CHAPTER 9

Aiding the Exodusters
97

CHAPTER 10

National Reactions to the Exodusters
109

CHAPTER 11

The Continued Search for Freedom
119

Chronology 127
Bibliography 130
Source Notes 132
Index 135

The Geography
of Hope

Black Exodus

1

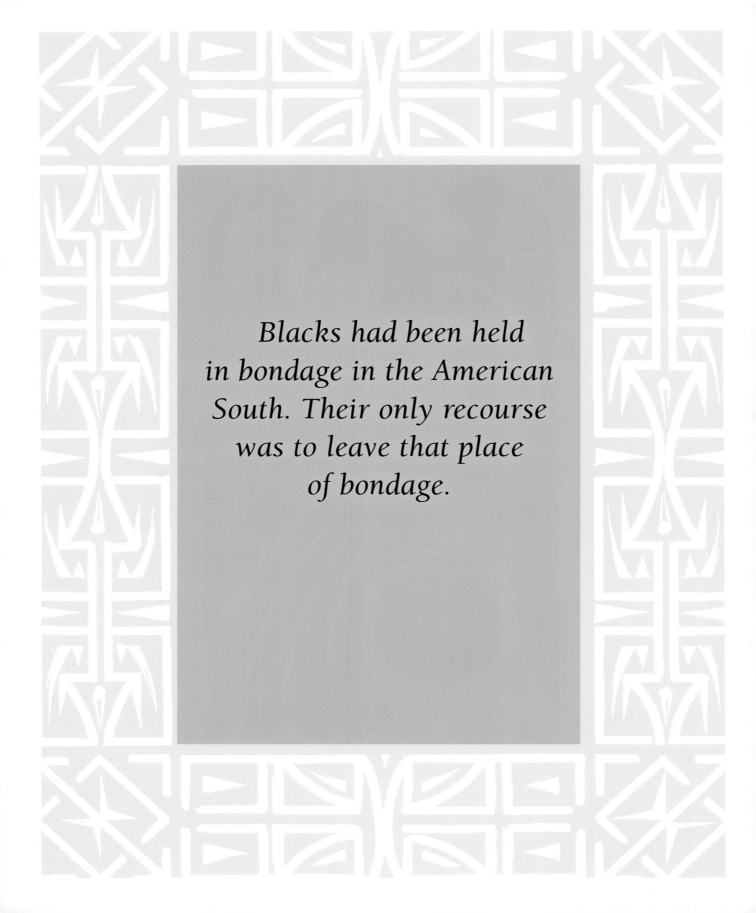

Blacks had been held in bondage in the American South. Their only recourse was to leave that place of bondage.

When the North emerged victorious from the Civil War, African Americans—slave and free—and whites who believed in true equality rejoiced in the hope of a society in which slavery would no longer exist and people, no matter what their color, would all enjoy the same basic rights. But thinking people of both races, in both the North and the South, realized that it would be very difficult for the nation to adjust to a new social order: Former slaves would need help in becoming self-sufficient, and their former masters—not to mention the poor whites who had based their sense of self-esteem on the fact that they were not black and not slaves—would resist any change in the social climate. These thinking people were right in their concerns. Far from accepting blacks—whether former slaves or lifelong freemen—into their society, most whites were determined to keep them in a servile position. Blacks in the North had long lived as second-class citizens; former slaves in the South soon learned that southern whites were determined to keep them in virtual slavery.

The vast majority of former slaves in the southern states had no option but to try to survive under circumstances that were not much different from those of slavery times. But in the first two decades after the Civil War, a comparatively small number of courageous (or determined or desperate) freedpeople chose instead to leave the South. Some went north, where they faced discrimination but not the grinding racism of the post-war South. A much larger number decided to head west, to the newly opened American frontier areas, following their dream of owning their own land and living from the fruits of their own labor. As such, they were following a distinctly American dream no different from that of a huge number of whites who pioneered in the western territories of the United States. But they were also following a biblical precedent, that of exodus from a land where they had been enslaved to a land where they could be free.

The western migration of southern blacks was a two-part movement. The first began even before the Civil War, and continued after it was over. It was a slow movement, made up of individuals and small groups who planned carefully for their relocation to the West and saved money for the move and the new lands they would occupy. The second was a spontaneous flight from violence and intimidation that was unplanned, unorganized, and large-scale enough to cause a temporary disruption of life in both the southern states from which the freedmen escaped and the western territories to which they fled.

The 20,000 or so blacks who were part of this spontaneous movement compared it to the biblical Exodus. The second book of the Old Testament, Exodus tells the story of how the Israelites, who had been held in bondage in Egypt, were led out of Egypt by Moses, to whom God had revealed Himself. They headed for the Promised Land of Canaan (ancient Palestine). Like the Israelites, blacks had been held in bondage in the American South and, in the post–Civil War era, even though slavery was officially abolished, remained virtual slaves; their only recourse was to leave that place of bondage. Since they were undertaking an exodus, they called themselves Exodusters. Like the biblical Exodus, the

14

Whether building pyramids for the Egyptians or picking cotton for the colonists, slavery is slavery. So it is natural that American slaves identified with their Israelite counterparts of 3,500 years earlier as described in the biblical book of Exodus.

Exoduster movement was a large relocation of an enslaved people. Unlike the Israelites, however, the Exodusters failed to find their promised land.

This book tells the story of both aspects of the westward migration during and after the Civil War years, and of three men who either encouraged, spurred, or led them.

The
Peculiar Institution

2

The social and political culture that had developed in the South depended on the existence of an unfree population.

Benjamin Singleton was born a slave in Davidson County, near Nashville, Tennessee, in 1809. Trained as a carpenter and cabinet maker, he probably had a life easier than that of most slaves, for he had a skill and was not forced to do the back-breaking agricultural work of field slaves. But for Singleton, life as a slave was no life at all, for he had no control over what happened to him.

When Singleton was born, the United States of America was a mere twenty-six years old, created by the people of thirteen British colonies who had declared their independence from Great Britain in 1776 and gone on to victory in a seven-year war for independence. Blacks, slave and free, had fought for the revolutionary cause, most in the hope that they were fighting for their own freedom as well as for that of whites. But when the former colonies set about organizing a government for their newly independent nation, they were unable to agree on what to do about slavery. While many people in the northern colonies believed that slavery was evil and had no place in a democratic country, most southerners were determined to maintain what historians have called "the peculiar institution." Southern colonies had come to depend on slave labor for their agricultural economies, and the social and political culture that had developed in the South depended on the existence of an unfree population at its bottom tier. Southern resistance to any change in that culture was so strong that the conflict of values threatened the formation of the new country. The framers of the United States Constitution did not even mention slavery in that document, referring instead to "persons owing labor."

But disputes between North and South did not end. Conflicts between southern and northern states over state's rights versus a strong federal government, and over the different needs of an agricultural versus an industrial economy, represented a serious threat to the continued union of the states. The issue of slavery was another point of conflict, especially as it concerned the admission of territories to the Union as new states. During the middle years of the nineteenth century, many attempts were made at compromise, but few compromises proved workable. Would-be new states became battlegrounds between pro- and anti-slavery forces.

Meanwhile, some courageous slaves took it upon themselves to secure their freedom by escaping slavery. Benjamin Singleton was among them. Sold to a master in New Orleans, he escaped and returned to Nashville, Tennessee. From there he made his way to Detroit, and then, according to some sources, to Canada, probably by way of the Underground Railroad.

Aided by this loosely organized network of whites and blacks, slave and free, who provided safe houses and passage for fugitives, many slaves, primarily from the Upper South like Singleton, were able to make their way to the North. The majority probably remained in the northern states, although they risked being re-enslaved. From the beginning of the new nation, laws had existed to deal with the problem of fugitive slaves. A Fugitive Slave Act passed in 1850 was the strongest yet, empowering federal officials to return escaped slaves to their masters

Runaway slaves were relentlessly pursued, not only by their masters to whom they represented monetary value, but also by federal officials empowered by the Fugitive Slave Act of 1850.

and decreeing that anyone helping fugitives could be arrested and fined so heavily that they would lose everything they owned. It was a contradiction for southern congressmen, who ordinarily championed state's rights against a powerful, central government, to lobby for this law. In response, many northern states, which generally favored more federal power, passed state laws aimed at protecting escaped slaves and those who aided them.

If Benjamin Singleton managed to reach Detroit, he probably did go farther north to Canada. Canada had long been a favored destination for fugitive slaves, for slavery was illegal in that British colony. By 1826 there were so many fugitive slaves living in Canada that plantation owners in Maryland and Kentucky asked U.S. Secretary of State Henry Clay to work out a plan with the Canadian government under which escaped slaves could be lawfully returned to their owners. Clay wrote to the Canadian government with this request, but the Canadians offered no help in returning the escaped slaves who were living within their borders.

Especially after the passage of the Fugitive Slave Act of 1850, Canada became the favored termination point of the journey. Many fugitives established organizations there to help those who followed. The Dawn Institute, located in Dresden, Ontario, which at that time was called Canada West, was formed in 1842 to teach fugitive slaves trades so they could support themselves in Canada. There were similar organizations in other Canadian communities along the Michigan border. It is not known what Benjamin Singleton did in Canada, but he evidently kept abreast of happenings in the United States and rejoiced when the Civil War broke out, believing that a Union victory would mean the end of slavery.

The election of Republican Abraham Lincoln as president in the fall of 1860 convinced white southern Democrats that their economy and their social and political values were in grave danger. In early 1861 seven southern states—Alabama, Florida, Georgia, Louisiana, Mississippi, South Carolina, and Texas—seceded from the Union and formed the Confederate States of America. After Confederate troops fired on the federal Fort Sumter in Charleston Harbor, South Carolina, President Lincoln issued a call for troops to defend the Union. His call caused four more southern states to secede and join the Confederacy: Arkansas, North Carolina, Virginia, and Benjamin Singleton's home state of Tennessee. Less than one hundred years after the British colonies of North America had fought their successful Revolution for independence and established the United States of America, the Union had collapsed, and the Civil War was on.

A small, tawny-colored man who could barely read, Benjamin Singleton was fifty-two years old when the Civil War began. Eager to return to the land of his birth, and confident that the Union would be victorious over the Confederacy, he anxiously followed news of events in the United States. After Union troops occupied Nashville in February 1862, Singleton returned to that city. He lived in a large Union camp for fugitive slaves along the river bank in Edgefield in East Nashville, and made a living building cabinets and coffins.

Outnumbered in population and lacking a navy, the Confederate States of America nevertheless waged a courageous and determined effort to save what southerners referred to as "the southern way of life." By this was meant its farming-based economy, its local political independence, and slavery. The Confederates held on for four long, bloody years, and their final defeat was due not only to their lack of a navy and heavy industry but also to the massive out-migration of its slaves.

Most northerners saw the war as a fight to preserve the Union. The issue of slavery was important, but not key. President Abraham Lincoln was not an abolitionist and was deeply concerned about what would happen if a large number of slaves were freed. But he understood that southern slaves were a significant factor in the South's arsenal. They provided much-needed labor to build fortifications, grow crops to feed Confederate troops, and do the noncombat work that was so important to support the combatants. In an effort to deprive the South of its valuable manual labor pool, Lincoln issued the Emancipation Proclamation, freeing the slaves in the Confederate states as of January 1, 1863.

The proclamation, presented to Congress in draft form in the fall of 1862, freed only the slaves in the Confederacy, because by law that was all Lincoln could do. Slaves were Confederate property, and it was his right as commander in chief of the Union forces to order the seizure of

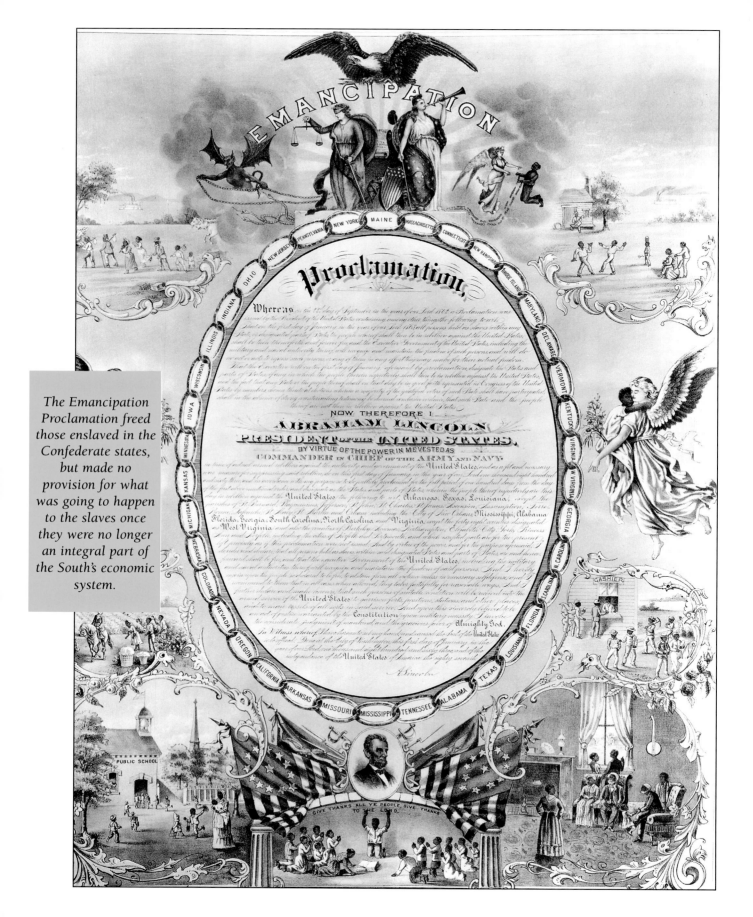

The Emancipation Proclamation freed those enslaved in the Confederate states, but made no provision for what was going to happen to the slaves once they were no longer an integral part of the South's economic system.

enemy property. He could not do the same for those slaves in the Union because the president of the United States had no constitutional right to act against slavery there. Thus, slaves remained in bondage in the slave-holding states that had stayed loyal to the Union, and the Confederate states lost one of the very rights that they had seceded from the Union to protect.

Confederates reacted predictably to the draft proclamation, refusing to be bound by it and declaring that it was not worth the paper it was written on. On October 10, Confederate President Jefferson Davis issued a call to the state of Virginia to draft 4,500 slaves to build fortifications around Richmond.

But blacks across the land rejoiced, certain that the proclamation was the first step toward the total emancipation of all slaves. Hundreds of slaves seized their freedom and made their way to Union encampments. Many abolitionists were especially excited over a provision in the Emancipation Proclamation providing that henceforth freed slaves "of suitable condition" would be "received into the armed service of the United States, to garrison forts, positions, stations, and other places, and to man vessels of all sorts in said service." The Union Army began to recruit companies of blacks, and black regiments soon played a significant role in the Union cause. But while a few black regiments were composed of former slaves, the majority comprised free blacks. Most freedpeople had no official status with the Union army.

The disruptions caused by the war were particularly difficult for southern slaves, whether or not they were theoretically free. Those who sought protection with Union troops were rarely welcomed with open arms by the Union officers who managed to occupy Confederate lands. Ill-clothed and ill-fed, they represented a burden for the military men, who resented the food they ate and the additional work the troops had to do to house and otherwise care for them, not to mention the delays caused in troop movements.

In the fall of 1864, Atlanta, Georgia, fell to the Union troops, and Union General William Tecumseh Sherman undertook a bold plan to "cut the Confederacy in half." In September, he began a 300-mile (483-kilometer) march to the sea, heading east from the vanquished city of

Freed slaves, known as "contrabands," fled their former life—but, in actuality, they had no place to go. Many tried to join the overcrowded camps of the Union armies, where their presence was considered a detriment to the war effort. Background: The promise was 40 acres and a mule—but the reality was something quite different as seen in this 1865 photo of a contraband camp at Richmond, Virginia.

Atlanta to Savannah, Georgia, cutting a path 50 to 60 miles (80 to 97 kilometers) wide, destroying crops, livestock, and houses. In the process, Sherman's troops uprooted thousands of slaves, and when those slaves sought refuge with the Union troops, many were turned away. Some were then recaptured and re-enslaved by Confederate forces. The resulting scandal in the North caused President Abraham Lincoln to send his secretary of war, Edwin Stanton, to Savannah to investigate. Stanton and Sherman met with twenty black ministers to listen to their complaints about how the slaves had been treated. The ministers argued that if given land, the former slaves could take care of themselves. Just days later, Sherman issued Field Order Number 15, setting aside more than 400,000 acres (160,000 hectares) of captured Confederate land and ordering that it be divided into small plots for the freed slaves. Each family would receive 40 acres (16 hectares) of land, and Sherman later provided for the army to assist the families by lending them mules.

Sherman regarded his official order as a simple method of relieving the political pressure he faced. He later claimed that the land grants were only a temporary measure for dealing with the freedmen and their families until the war was over, and that he had never promised to convey permanent possession of the land. During the Reconstruction period that followed the war, most of the lands granted the freedmen and their families were taken away.

The idea that all freedpeople's households were to have had 40 acres and a mule, courtesy of the federal government, persists to this day, and has contributed greatly to the general sense of betrayal felt by African Americans. At no time was that sense of betrayal more keenly felt than during Reconstruction, when freedmen gradually became aware that the promises of Emancipation were empty ones and that their hopes for a new life farming on their own land—or of enjoying even the most basic rights—were not to be realized if they remained in the South.

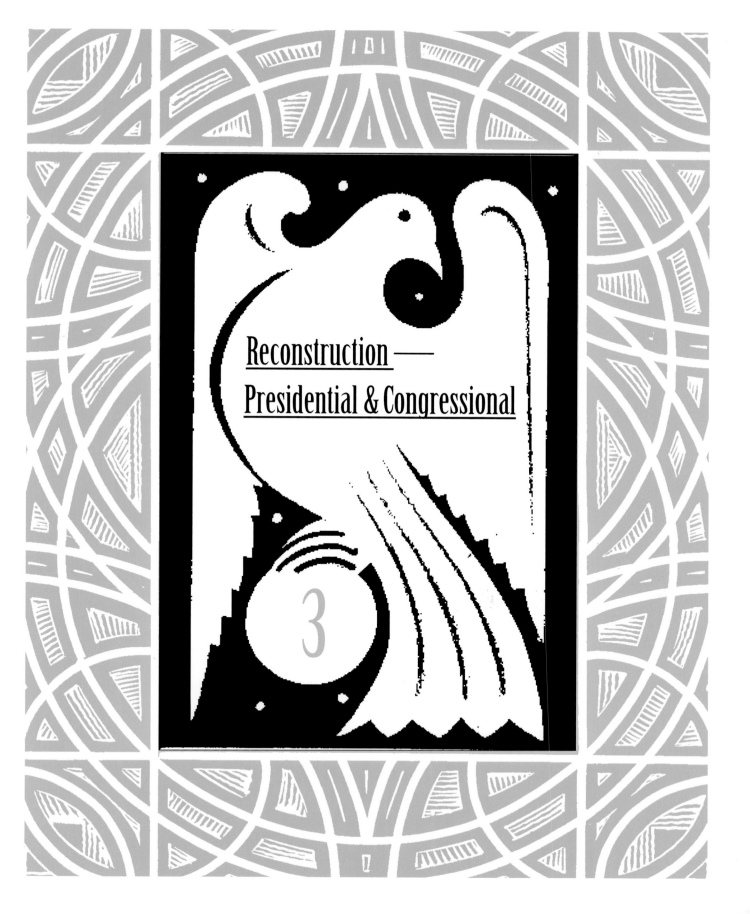

Reconstruction —
Presidential & Congressional

The former slaves remained in virtual slavery, working for whites and getting little or nothing in return.

By the time he had issued the Emancipation Proclamation, President Lincoln was quite certain that the North would be victorious in the Civil War. With the reconstitution of the Union still his primary goal, he had already formulated a plan to bring the former rebel states back into the fold. He began to institute his plan long before the war ended, in areas that Union troops had seized, such as the Sea Islands off the coast of the Carolinas, Nashville and other parts of Tennessee, and New Orleans. Lincoln formalized his plans for reuniting the Union in his Proclamation of Amnesty and Reconstruction, delivered in December 1863, some sixteen months before the war ended.

Under his plan, Federal troops would occupy the former Confederate states until such time as those states sought readmission to the Union.

Readmission would be granted if 10 percent of a state's voters took an oath of loyalty to the Union. Lincoln did not make black suffrage, or the granting to blacks of the right to vote, a condition for a state's readmission. Indeed, he was not sure what should be done about the freedpeople. Assassinated just days after the war's end in April 1865, Lincoln had little influence on Reconstruction policies as they actually played out. Lincoln's vice president, Andrew Johnson, assumed the presidency after Lincoln's death.

Just before the end of the war, Congress passed a bill creating the Bureau of Freedmen, Refugees, and Abandoned Lands, whose purpose was to assist freed slaves throughout the South. Originally designed to be a one-year "bridge" from slavery to freedom, the Federal Freedmen's Bureau operated in the South until 1869, and its educational activities continued for another three years. The Bureau distributed rations to the needy and helped organize the first public schools in the South as well as churches and medical facilities. Essentially, it functioned as the government in the South. It was the only court of appeal for black people, and its records, held at the National Archives in Washington, D.C., contain voluminous correspondence about freedmen held in virtual slavery, freedmen asking for help in finding family members who had been sold away from them during slavery, and acts of violence against blacks.

Henry Adams was twenty-two years old when the Civil War ended in 1865. One of about sixty slaves on a plantation in Louisiana, he was summoned with the others to hear some momentous news. Adams later recalled: "The white men read a paper to all of us colored people telling us that we were free and could go where we pleased and work for who we pleased. The man I belonged to told me it was best to stay with him. He said, 'The bad white men was mad with the Negroes because they were free and they would kill you all for fun.' He said, stay where we are living and we could get protection from our old masters.

"I told him I thought that every man, when he was free, could have his rights and protect themselves."[1]

Adams's former master insisted that his way was best, but Adams was not persuaded. In fact, he suspected that "the white people is trying to fool us." But Adams had nowhere to go, and no means to make a living,

In addition to its political and educational functions, the Freedmen's Bureau was the only court of appeal for black people, because blacks could rarely get a fair trial in Southern courts. Unfortunately, the bureau's authority was usually too limited to ensure justice.

An 1865 lithograph portraying a scene that occurred on plantations throughout the vanquished Confederacy—a white man reading the Emancipation Proclamation to slaves—while simultaneously warning them of the cruel world that awaited them and assuring them that staying where they were was in their best interest.

33

and so he remained on his old plantation. He did not, however, sign the labor contract "the boss" offered to him. Of all the former slaves on his plantation, only Adams and one other man refused to sign.

Actually, such labor contracts were instituted not by southern planters but by the Federal troops that occupied Louisiana and other parts of the former Confederacy. The purpose of such contracts, in the minds of the occupying administrators, was to ensure that former slaves had at least some rights and would henceforth be compensated for their labor. Adams recalled his former master saying, "Sign this contract so I can take it to the Yankees and have it recorded."

But most former slaves, unable to read or write, had no idea what sort of document they were putting their "X" to. The contracts, as explained by Henry Adams's boss and other bosses, provided for people to work for the year and at the end of the year be entitled to a share of the profits from the crop, generally anywhere from one-fifth to one-third. But the bosses did not plan to keep their end of the bargain, and the contracts were not worth the paper they were written on. White plantation owners and other white bosses had no intention of making fair labor contracts with the former slaves. Their only concern was that the people remain with them, for black labor was essential if the South was to rebuild.

In effect, then, the former slaves remained in virtual slavery, working for whites and getting little or nothing in return.

Other aspects of slavery continued as well. Henry Adams told what happened when he asked the boss for permission to go to Shreveport. "He said, 'You better carry a pass.' I said, 'I will see whether I am free by going without a pass.'"

Adams continued, "I met four white men about six miles south of Keachie, De Soto Parish. One of them asked me who I belonged to. I told him no one. So him and two others struck me with a stick and told me they were going to kill me and every other Negro who told them that they did not belong to anyone." Fortunately for Adams, one of the men knew him and told his companions to leave him alone. Others were not so lucky. Adams recalled, "I seen over twelve colored men and women, beat, shot and hung between there and Shreveport."[2]

Returning to his home plantation, Adams learned that he did not even have the right to call his boss "boss" rather than "master." On arrival, Adams found that his boss was not at home, and so he asked "the madame" where he was. According to Adams, she went into a rage, saying, "Now, the boss; now, the boss! You should say 'master' and 'mistress'—and shall or leave. We will not have no nigger here on our place who cannot say 'mistress' and 'master.' You all are not free yet and will not be until Congress sits, and you shall call every white lady 'missus' and every white man 'master.'"[3]

Congress went back into formal session that fall of 1865. One of the first items on its agenda was the passage of the Thirteenth Amendment to the Constitution, abolishing slavery. The amendment was then presented to the states for ratification by a two-thirds majority. There was much to be done to "reconstruct" the former Confederate states. These states would have to swear allegiance to the Union and pass their own laws guaranteeing rights to the former slaves. At first, Congress allowed President Johnson to take the lead in developing a Reconstruction plan.

A Tennesseean like Benjamin Singleton, a tailor by trade and self-educated, Johnson had been a U.S. senator from Tennessee when the Civil War began. He had long resented the large slaveholders who had held power in his region, and when Tennessee had seceded from the Union, he had remained in his seat in the Senate, the only senator from a seceding state to do so. Senator Johnson's loyalty to the Union had led Lincoln to select him as his running mate in the 1864 presidential election.

Johnson basically followed Lincoln's plan. He demanded that the former Confederate states hold new constitutional conventions at which southern whites who had received amnesty would amend their constitutions to nullify the ordinances of secession, ratify the Thirteenth Amendment to the U.S. Constitution, and repudiate Confederate debts. Under the easy terms of what later came to be called Presidential Reconstruction, the former Confederate states proceeded quickly to rejoin the Union.

Ensuring a return to economic normalcy was as important to the South as rejoining the Union and "getting back to normal" politically. To guarantee that the former slaves continued to function as the South's labor force, southern legislators passed a series of rigid labor-control laws called "Black Codes." Although they differed from state to state, most of these codes had the same basic provisions: If a freedman were found without "lawful employment," he could be arrested and jailed or fined. If he could not pay the fine, he could be hired out to a white employer who would deduct the fine from the worker's wages. Other provisions prevented blacks from engaging in any employment other than agricultural or domestic.

There were other degradations. Although most labor contracts specified that employers were not to beat their workers, many kept doing so. While, theoretically, the freedmen could now enter into legal marriage contracts, they were not allowed to live together as man and wife. And when former slaves left their home plantations, they were not allowed to return to visit their relatives.

Henry Adams refused to accept such treatment. After his former mistress and master beat his fifteen-year-old sister nearly to death, a number of the young black men on the plantation determined to leave the place. Adams, his brother, and ten other young men headed for Shreveport. Along the way, some forty whites attacked them and robbed them of all their money and possessions. Adams refused to return to his home plantation. He secured a wagon and started peddling goods, but had to get a pass from the parish to do so. But the pass did not protect him from marauding bands of white men, whose mission was to keep "the niggers in their place."

Like Henry Adams, Benjamin Singleton was witness to the degradations of the freedpeople at the hands of their former owners. Working for an undertaker in Nashville, he heard many tales of hardships. As Singleton testified before Congress in 1880, he grew tired of hearing the former slaves' tales of unfair treatment by whites:

"These men would tell all their grievances to me in Tennessee—the sorrows of their heart. . . . Well, actually, I would have to go and bury their fathers and mothers. You see we have the same heart and feelings as any other race and nation. (The land is free, and it is nobody's business, if there is land enough, where the people go. I put that in my people's heads.) Well, that man would die, and I would bury him; and the

A Thomas Nast lithograph showing the mockery that was being made of the Emancipation Proclamation in the South as a black boy is sold from the pedestal of a statue called Liberty, and a black man is beaten at the base of another statue called Justice.

If the leadership of the Exoduster movement could be credited to one individual, it would no doubt be Benjamin "Pap" Singleton, whose name constantly intertwines with the effort to find a means of "life, liberty, and the pursuit of happiness" for his people.

next morning maybe a woman would go to that man (meaning the land-lord), and she would have six or seven children, and he would say to her, 'Well, your husband owed me before he died' and they would say that to every last one of them, 'You owe me.' Suppose he would? Then he would say, 'You must go to some other place; I cannot take care of you.' Now, you see, that is something I would take notice of, that woman had to go out, and these little children was left running through the streets, and the next place you would find them in a disorderly house, and their children in the State's prison."[4]

Singleton and Adams were not alone in being enraged by the treatment of the freedpeople. The passage of Black Codes in the former Rebel states convinced many Republicans in Congress that the southern governments were flouting the purpose of Reconstruction and the Thirteenth Amendment, and showing insufficient repentance for the sin of seceding from the Union. Both Radical and moderate Republicans joined in refusing to seat the newly elected southern representatives and established a joint committee to investigate the situation in the South. Learning from wide-ranging testimony by army officers, white southern Unionists, Freedmen's Bureau officials, and a few freedpeople that the southern states were engaging in the systematic oppression of blacks, Congress took steps to protect them and reassert federal control over the former Confederate states. Their actions would be referred to as Radical Reconstruction.

In 1867, Congress passed the first Reconstruction Act, which divided the former Confederacy into five military districts, required the former Confederate states to hold new elections for state office, and also declared that voting rights were available to all male citizens regardless of "race or previous condition of servitude." The effect of that last provision was to give blacks a majority vote in most southern states. The first legal voting by a black man was recorded later that year in New Orleans, Lousiana.

Congress also passed a bill extending the life of the Freedmen's Bureau and expanded its powers. It then passed the Civil Rights Bill, granting freedpeople the "full and equal benefit of all laws." An enraged President Johnson vetoed both bills, but Congress overrode his vetoes, the first time in American history that a major piece of legislation was passed over the veto of the chief executive. Congress then proceeded to ensure its guarantee of civil rights for southern blacks by passing the Fourteenth constitutional amendment, which granted full citizenship to blacks and prohibited states from denying them equal protection of the laws. All these laws ushered in what came to be called Radical Reconstruction.

Henry Adams enlisted in the Army, serving with the occupying federal troops in Louisiana. That service gave him the opportunity to see what the federal government was trying to do for the freedmen and freedwomen. Adams also observed how the Reconstruction government in his state—whose representatives included a number of blacks and northerners, since any southerner who could be proved to have aided the Confederacy could not hold office—tried, but usually failed, to create better conditions for the former slaves. Adams wondered if there was any state in the former Confederacy where the freedmen were truly free.

Many white southerners were infuriated by Radical Reconstruction. The Ku Klux Klan began to grow rapidly. Founded by former Confederate soldiers in Pulaskie, Tennessee, in 1866, the Ku Klux Klan was a secret society with mysterious codes and hooded robes and a fierce determination to maintain "white supremacy." As it grew, it became more and more violent, holding night parades, burning crosses, and engaging in beatings and lynchings of blacks and their white sympathizers.

The Klan was particularly effective in preventing southern blacks from exercising their newly acquired right to vote, and it was in part because of Klan terrorist activities that, beginning in 1870, Congress passed a series of Enforcement Acts aimed at controlling the Klan and guaranteeing civil and political rights for blacks. That same year, Congress approved the Fifteenth Amendment to the Constitution, which declared that the right of male citizens of the United States to vote could not "be denied or abridged" by any state "on account of race, color, or previous condition of servitude." In April 1871, following a particular spate of violence in the small town of Meridien, Mississippi, Congress passed the Ku Klux Klan Act, declaring certain individual

This wood engraving from Harper's *Weekly* shows freedmen, among them a Union veteran, casting their votes for the first time. The malevolence in the eyes of the poll watcher seems a harbinger of things to come....

The joy of freedom paled against the terror that black families must have felt as the hooded members of the Ku Klux Klan carried out their nighttime campaigns of murder and brutality.

crimes against citizens' rights to be punishable by federal law. Later in the same year, the new president, former Union general Ulysses S. Grant, declared martial law in parts of the Carolinas and Mississippi, dispatching federal troops to quell the violence.

Henry Adams's army enlistment was up in 1870, the same year that Congress passed the Enforcement Acts. He and some of the other blacks who had served with him resolved to ascertain what Adams called "the true condition of our race."

Members of the group, which they called "the Committee," fanned out across the South. "We worked our way from place to place and from State to State," Adams later recalled, "and worked amongst our people in the fields to see what sort of living our people lived. We wanted to see whether there was any State in the South where we could get a living and enjoy our rights. At one time there was five hundred of us. About one hundred and fifty went from one place to another. The information they brought to us was very bad."

Adams saw firsthand how whites cheated their black workers:

"I picked cotton at the Forster plantation and I seen the white men that weighed the cotton. When the draught would weigh seventy-five pounds they would check fifty pounds. Yet they were charging colored people fifteen and twenty-one cents per pound for meat; ten pounds of flour for $1. . . I worked on James Hollingsworth's plantation and the same thing was practiced on that place. On Dr. Vance's plantation where I often worked, I have seen the same. From the mouth of Red River to Jefferson, Texas, no difference can be seen. Even in Arkansas and Texas where I traveled I see the same, as it was my business to look around and ascertain as far as possible into the treatment of colored people by whites.

"In going from Shreveport to New Orleans I seen along the banks of Red River colored people who were afraid to talk to me at landings. I asked several of them, 'Do you not live well?' They told me, 'No, the whites take all we make and if we say anything about our rights they beat us.'"[5]

Adams advised them to go from plantation to plantation until they found a boss who would be fair to them. But the people believed that all whites were the same, and that moving around would do no good.

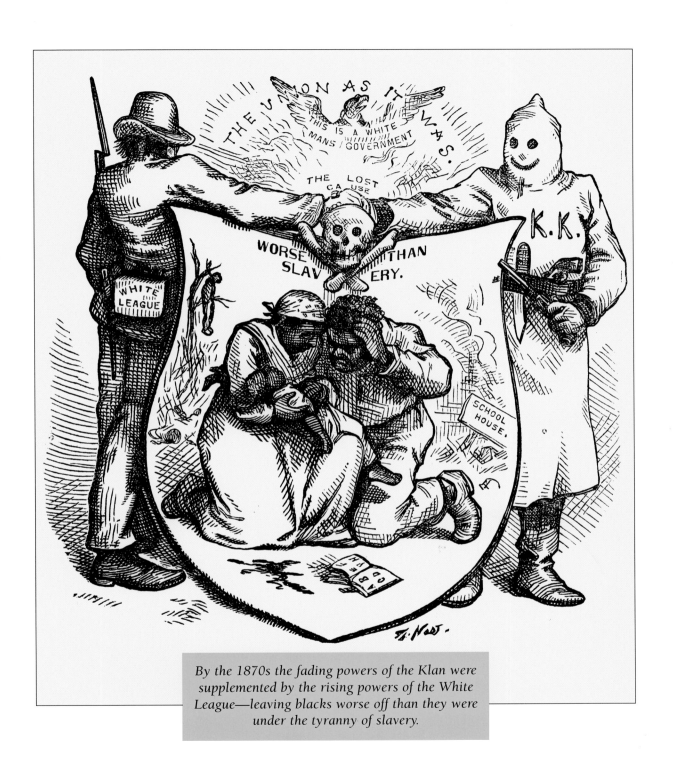

By the 1870s the fading powers of the Klan were supplemented by the rising powers of the White League—leaving blacks worse off than they were under the tyranny of slavery.

With all of the forces working against him, including his own government, it is little wonder that Henry Adams gave up on trying to work through the system in the form of the Joint Select Committee to Inquire into the Condition of the State of Affairs in the Late Insurrectionary States.

Adams's committee documented their findings and in a short time had pages and pages of testimony. But the question was, what to do with it? They believed there was no point in taking their case to the black politicians who were enjoying a brief moment of influence in the Reconstruction governments. Adams's committee didn't even include any black politicians. As he later explained, "No politicianers didn't belong to it because we was afraid that if we allowed the colored politicianer to belong he would tell it to the Republican politicianer and, from that, the men that was doing all this to us would get after us."[6]

The Committee sent its findings to the U.S. Congress in Washington, D.C., which formed a Joint Select Committee to Inquire into the Condition of Affairs in the Late Insurrectionary States. That committee began to hold hearings in 1872.[7]

Although Adams and the other members of the Committee continued to distrust politicians, they did involve themselves in local politics. Adams, who had gotten a job as a railsplitter and plantation manager for the W. C. Hambleton Company, voted for the first time in 1870. Approached by many blacks in Caddo Parish for his views, he demurred, saying he was merely a "rail-splitter and wood-chopper" and knew nothing of politics. He did, however, suggest that the Democrats were no friends of the freedmen.[8] Adams later learned that he had been "spotted" and that local whites had marked him for assassination. But Adams refused to stop speaking up.

In the early 1870s, local whites who were determined to restore Louisiana to its prewar political and social status formed the White League. Among the activities of the White League was exerting pressure on employers not to employ troublesome blacks, and Henry Adams lost his job. According to Adams, W. C. Hambleton told him, "Adams, I think a heap of you as a man; I know you are a true man, and that you will do what you promise to do, but under this order I cannot employ you. . . . You are a good old Republican, and I cannot employ you because you are a Republican. I cannot employ you no more."[9]

By 1872, Adams had been hired to manage the wood yard and its workers on a plantation outside Shreveport. Within a year, he had been given the added responsibilities of purchasing the cotton seed and corn and running the cotton-oil machine. In 1873, he was selected from the voter rolls to serve on a grand jury in Shreveport, along with nine other black men and six whites. In that position, he got to see at first hand that the local justice system was no fairer to blacks than it had been under slavery.

Although ten blacks served on that grand jury, the judge, lawyers, and clerk were all white, and they clearly favored the whites in all the cases that came before them. Whereas a white accused of a crime was allowed to remain free unless he or she was indicted, or formally charged, blacks—men, women, and children—were jailed before they were indicted. Adams wrote to the Senate committee, "I saw little colored boys in there for stealing one can of oysters. I seen little girls in there for stealing such things as thimbles, scissors, &c., and [there] was several colored men in prison, and only two white men were put in jail for crimes they had committed. . . ."[10] The blacks were usually indicted, almost always convicted, and—whether women or men—they were ordinarily sent to the chain gang. During his grand jury service, Adams saw many black women come before the court, but no white women. In all the cases considered in the year 1873, only one white man was indicted for killing a black man in cold blood, and he was eventually found not guilty.

By the summer of 1874, the activities of the White League had become such a threat to the state government's authority that Republican Governor William Pitt Kellogg asked for federal troops to help put down White League activity in several Louisiana parishes. Adams's committee also sent a petition to President Grant and to Congress in September, asking for help. In response, the Seventh Cavalry went to Shreveport to try to reassert order. In March 1875, Henry Adams went to work for the Seventh Cavalry as an undercover agent, reporting on White League excesses against local blacks. But it was dangerous work, and secrecy was far more crucial than it was for his activities with the Committee. He lasted only three months. Having spent years documenting the freedmen's sorrows, certain that if the government only knew what was going on it would step in to help, Henry Adams at last gave up. By 1875, he and other members of the Committee had ceased their operations.

Reconstruction
Ends

4

Northerners lost interest in the cause of human rights.

All efforts on the part of the federal government to "reconstruct" the South had proved unavailing, and as time went on became more and more halfhearted.

A major distraction for Congress was the Panic of 1873, triggered by the collapse of one of the country's largest investment houses, Jay Cooke and Company. Within days, several banks had closed, and the New York Stock Exchange shut down for more than a week—the first time the exchange had ever closed. Thousands of businesses went bankrupt, putting hundreds of thousands of people out of work. By 1874, the number of people unemployed because of the depression was estimated at one million. In northern cities, which had become more and more dependent on industrialization, the problem of unemployment was especially severe. Thousands of the unemployed took to the roads in search of work. By 1876, when America celebrated the hundredth anniversary of its independence, the nation was in the fourth year of the depression.

In the South, economic hardship drove many black renters back into the ranks of sharecroppers or laborers and sharply reduced their wages. In the North, businessmen blamed the economic paralysis of the South, which they believed was caused by Radical Reconstruction, for the national depression. Wrote a New York businessman in 1875, "What the South now needs is capital to develop her resources, but this she cannot obtain till confidence in her state governments can be restored, and this will never be done by federal bayonets. We have tried this long enough. Now let the South alone."[11]

In the face of economic depression, attempts to reconstruct the former Confederate states so that they would become places of equality for all fell by the wayside. Northerners lost interest in the cause of human rights when their pocketbooks were empty. In response, unrepentant southerners seized the moment and worked to ensure the resurgence of white rule.

First, white southern Democrats drove white southern Republicans from the Republican Party, making it impossible for a Republican to live and prosper in the South. Simultaneously, the Democrats instituted measures to prevent blacks, who were solidly Republican, from voting. Through intimidation and outright violence, they kept blacks from the polls. In Mississippi, Democrats had retaken power by 1875. They then devised the "Mississippi Plan" for being readmitted to the Union, a plan that became a model for other southern states.

Whereas in previous years, the Republican administration in Washington, D.C., would have taken steps to end this violence—by sending federal troops back to the South, if necessary—now President Grant did nothing. He had taken the political pulse of the times. Northerners, whether businessmen or working-class people, had tired of the turmoil of Reconstruction. Blaming Republicans for the national depression, many voted for northern Democrats in the elections of 1874, with the result that Democrats took control of the House of

The violence was so widespread during the election for the governorship of Mississippi in November 1865 that federal troops were requested to protect black voters from white gangs. President Grant refused to send them, indicating that the public was tired of such outbreaks in the South.

Representatives. By the presidential election of 1876, the vote for the Republican candidate, Rutherford B. Hayes, and the Democratic contender, Samuel J. Tilden, was so close that only a secret compromise ensured the unchallenged victory of Hayes. In return for Democratic support, Republicans were forced to promise to remove all remaining federal troops from the South. By April 1877, Hayes had kept the Republican promise, pulling out the last remaining federal troops from the capitals of Louisiana and South Carolina, leaving the way clear for Democrats to regain power.

Echoing the feelings of the northern businessman quoted above, the Democrats emphasized (and the rest of the nation agreed) that the country's financial crisis was due in large measure to the political and economic paralysis of the South, and that the sooner life could return to normal in that part of the country, the better off the entire country would be. Declare the South "redeemed," they argued. Leave it alone. And if that meant abandoning black southerners to the wrath and resentment of their former owners, so be it.

And so "redemption" was declared complete, and as Democrats took control of the southern states through the 1870s, Black Codes were reinstituted and the provisions of the Thirteenth and Fourteenth Amendments were effectively nullified by the institution of literacy requirements, poll taxes, and other discriminatory voter-registration laws.

To today's ears, it is ironic that a term with religious overtones, like *redemption*, should be applied to a political and economic situation. But the late nineteenth century was a time of religious revival, and the term came easily to the lips of many. By the same token, it was biblical terminology that came to the lips of frustrated blacks who saw no hope for southern blacks.

Frederick Douglass, a former slave who had escaped to the North and become a leading abolitionist and spokesman for blacks, had rejoiced over Emancipation and the promise of Reconstruction. But he had also witnessed the tragedy of the postwar era. He cited the historical precedents of other freed peoples in summing up the broken promise of Reconstruction:

The eloquence that Frederick Douglass had used so effectively to advocate freedom of the slaves was used even more effectively to decry the injustices of the Reconstructionist era.

You say you have emancipated us. You have; and I thank you for it. But what is your emancipation?

When the Israelites were emancipated they were told to go and borrow of their neighbors—borrow their coin, borrow their jewels, load themselves down with the means of subsistence; after, they should go free in the land which the Lord God gave them. When the Russian serfs had their chains broken and given their liberty, the government of Russia—aye, the despotic government of Russia—gave to those poor emancipated serfs a few acres of land on which they could live and earn their bread.

But when you turned us loose, you gave us no acres. You turned us loose to the sky, to the storm, to the whirlwind, and, worst of all, you turned us loose to the wrath of our infuriated masters.[12]

The only alternative, it seemed to many blacks, also had its precedent in the Bible: Exodus.

To Find
a Place to Live Free

5

*Many southern
black groups concluded
that emigration was
the only course.*

Some Southern blacks moved North.

As early as December 31, 1865, only eight months after the Union victory, the *South Carolina Leader*, a black newspaper in Charleston, reported: "It is ascertained that 3,200 freedmen have emigrated from this State during the last three months, to Mass., Conn., and other New England states on contracts to work at $20 a month; and they are still going. Thousands are going from Virginia, and yet the supply is inadequate to the demand. . . ."[13]

But for men like Henry Adams, migration to the North was not the answer. He and his fellow Committee members in Louisiana reformed themselves as the Colonization Council and vowed to lobby the federal government to set aside a separate territory for blacks within U.S. borders. In late December 1875, Adams accompanied a delegation of black ministers to New Orleans to attend a conference of representatives from several southern states, including Alabama, Arkansas, Mississippi, and Texas. At that conference, Adams learned that the exploitation of blacks was not confined to Louisiana, Arkansas, and other areas where the Committee had conducted investigations, and that in fact it was widespread across the South. The delegates declared that the South was just not a place for black people and discussed several alternatives, including emigration to other U.S. territories and Liberia.

Adams was especially intrigued by the idea of emigration to Liberia, which had been created on the West Coast of Africa by the American Colonization Society (ACS). Founded in Washington, D.C., in the winter of 1816–1817, the American Colonization Society was a white organization whose members believed the best course for free blacks in the United States was to return to their native land. They were aided indirectly by Congress when in 1819 that legislative body appropriated $100,000 for returning to Africa blacks who had been brought to the United States illegally after the slave trade was abolished in the United States. In 1821, agents of the ACS purchased from local De chiefs land on Africa's Atlantic coast—an area called Cape Mesurado, bordered on the northwest by Sierra Leone, on the north by Guinea, and on the east by the Ivory Coast. The colony's name, Liberia, meant "place of freedom or liberty."

The American Colonization Society transported the first black settlers to Liberia in 1822, and over the next several decades some 15,000 American blacks emigrated there. Most free blacks in the United States had no interest in "repatriation," however. As a group of free people of color in Richmond, Virginia, protested in January 1817, shortly after the American Colonization Society was founded, they preferred to be "colonized in the most remote corner of the land of our nativity, to being exiled" in Africa.[14]

Eleven years later, at a meeting of the New York African Society for Mutual Relief in 1828, New Yorker Thomas L. Jennings (1791–1859) expressed similar sentiments:

"Our relation with Africa is the same as the white man's is with Europe. We have passed through several generations in this country and

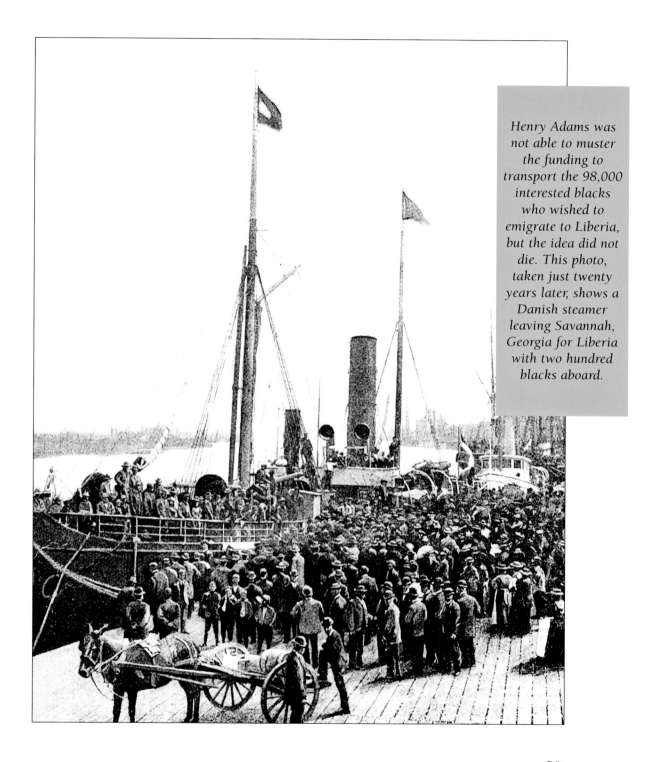

Henry Adams was not able to muster the funding to transport the 98,000 interested blacks who wished to emigrate to Liberia, but the idea did not die. This photo, taken just twenty years later, shows a Danish steamer leaving Savannah, Georgia for Liberia with two hundred blacks aboard.

consequently have become naturalized. Our habits, our manners, our passions, our dispositions have become the same. . . . I might as well tell the white man about England, France or Spain, the country from whence his forefathers emigrated, and call him a European, as for him to call us Africans. Africa is as foreign to us as Europe is to them."[15]

Unfortunately for Henry Adams and the other delegates to the 1875 conference in New Orleans, no federal help was available to transport blacks to Liberia. For the time being, he urged, the delegates should go back to their home states and do all they could to work for a Republican victory in the 1876 elections.

But by 1876, southern blacks were so demoralized by the climate of violence—and by experiences of white persecution they'd suffered or had been suffered by people they knew—and so fearful of reprisals should they attempt to work for—or even vote for—Republican candidates, that they were loath to follow Adams's urging. The outcome of the election of 1876 in Louisiana was a Democratic takeover of the state government, followed the next year by the withdrawal of all federal troops from the South, which was declared "redeemed." Henry Adams turned much of his energies toward colonization.

The Colonization Council sent representatives to emigration meetings and gathered the names of local blacks who wished to leave the South. According to Adams, 98,000 people—mostly Louisianans, but also people from Texas, Arkansas, and Mississippi—enrolled on the lists. Adams began to correspond with the American Colonization Society. He was not alone. The society was contacted at that time by many southern black groups that had concluded that emigration was the only course. But the society informed all who wrote that it did not have the money to send thousands of blacks to Liberia, and that the local organizations would have to raise the necessary funds. Adams's Colonization Society tried to institute a system of dues, but they were rarely able to collect from the poor sharecroppers whose exploitation by white landlords was so severe that they could barely provide for their own families. At a meeting of the National Colored Colonization Society in Shreveport, Louisiana, in September 1877, a petition was sent to President Rutherford B. Hayes asking that money be appropriated for Liberian emigration. But no funds were forthcoming.

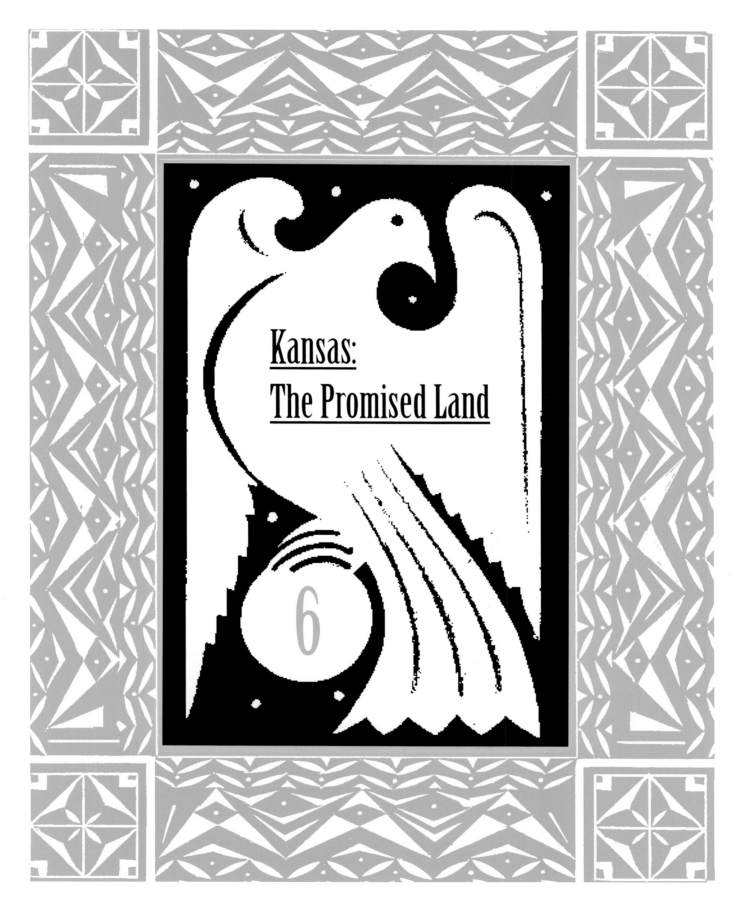

Kansas:
The Promised Land

6

Blacks looked to Kansas as a place where they could enjoy freedom.

Like Henry Adams, Benjamin "Pap" Singleton also held out hope, for a time, that Tennessee Republicans would be able to stave off the growing Democratic threat. In the meantime, he had also begun exploring other alternatives to remaining in virtual slavery. Unlike Adams, Singleton probably never seriously considered emigration to Liberia. Instead, he pursued the notion of homesteading on unsettled land.

As he was quoted in the St. Louis *Globe-Democrat* in 1879, complete with the reporter's attempts at rendering southern dialect, Singleton explained, "It was ag'in nature for the masters and the slaves to jine hands and work together. Nuthin' but de millinium could bring that around. The whites had the lands and the sense, an' the blacks had nothin' but their freedom,—an' it was just like a dream to 'em."[16]

At first, Singleton promoted the notion of settling in frontier areas of Tennessee. But it was not long before he had set his sights on Kansas. Free blacks had established settlements in frontier areas since the late 1810s. At the time, the "frontier" included Illinois and Ohio. While some of those settlements were founded by blacks, several were so-called manumission settlements, created by whites who had freed their slaves. The will of one John Randolph directed that land be purchased in Mercer County, Ohio, for this purpose. Randolph's will stated, "I give and bequeath to all my slaves their freedom—heartily regretting that I have ever been the owner of one." Randolph's will also provided for money to pay his former slaves' transportation to Ohio, as well as the basic necessities, such as clothing, shelter, and tools, to begin their new lives. In 1832, 385 of Randolph's former slaves arrived in Mercer County, traveling first by wagon and then by boat, only to find that Randolph's relatives had successfully contested his will and secured the land for themselves. Although the whites of the area shunned the stranded freed-people at first, they eventually took pity on them and gave them jobs so they could provide for themselves. Many remained in Ohio, while others headed farther west, into Indiana.

In the same year that John Randolph's former slaves arrived in Ohio, blacks and Cherokee Indians from Northampton County, North Carolina, arrived in Hamilton County, Indiana, to establish a settlement. Like blacks in many other areas of the country, these North Carolina blacks had settled among the Indians, and when the state of North Carolina carried out an "Indian removal," the blacks accompanied their friends. The settlement they established in Indiana was called the Roberts Settlement, after "Long James" Roberts, one of the black settlers. This community thrived.

There were also instances in which enterprising individual blacks sought to establish frontier settlements. In 1836, a freedman named Frank McWorter (1777–1854), who preferred to call himself simply Free Frank, established a town in Pike County on the Illinois frontier. He purchased land, divided it into lots, and sold them, primarily to other blacks. He named his town New Philadelphia, after the city in Pennsylvania that was at the time a leading urban center for free blacks.

New Philadelphia attracted settlers and thrived as an agricultural marketing center. Its location on an important country road leading to the Mississippi River and its flourishing steamboat trade contributed to its early growth and success. But when the railroad came through Pike County for the first time in 1869, it bypassed New Philadelphia, and the town did not survive.

More than anything else, the railroad built the modern nation of the United States by connecting the two distinct areas of American population that existed when the Civil War broke out. The first, and older, population center was the land from the Atlantic coast to the states west of the Mississippi River. The other, and newer, was from the Sierra Nevada mountains to the Pacific coast. In between was a vast expanse of land that was occupied primarily by Native American Indians. The only way to cross that expanse was by wagon train, a slow process fraught with dangers—from inclement weather, prairie fires, and hostile Indians.

The best hope for communication between the two settled areas, and for development of the territories in between, was the railroad, many lines of which had already been built in the settled areas. In 1862, while the Civil War was raging, Congress had authorized the charter of the Union Pacific and Central Pacific railroad corporations to construct a line between Omaha, Nebraska, and Sacramento, California. Each company would begin at the edge of the great divide that separated them, and work toward the other. That crucial cross-continental link was completed in 1869, when a golden spike was hammered into place at Promontory Point, Utah. Other railroad companies were busy constructing a web of tracks throughout the underserved areas. In the six years between 1867 and 1873, some 35,000 miles of track were laid, more than had been built in the thirty years before the Civil War.

Huge government subsidies made this railroad expansion possible. Congress gave public land to the railroad companies—more than 100 million acres altogether—and also provided loans and tax breaks to encourage the growth of the continental transportation system.

Recognizing that the railroads would be useless without settlements and towns along their routes, Congress passed the Homestead Act in 1862, the same year that it authorized the transcontinental rail link.

Many black leaders believed that the vacant, government-owned lands of the West would be the ideal place to resettle the former slaves of the South. They vigorously pressed their cause in the halls of the federal government. But that idea didn't sit well with most Congressmen, who decided it was best to make the land available to all.

Theoretically, the Homestead Act enabled any citizen or permanent immigrant to obtain 160 acres (65 hectares) of public land for a fee of $10, and to claim final title to the land after five years of residence. In practice, few individual Americans had the resources even to afford the $10 fee, not to mention the money to pay to get to the West and to buy the necessary equipment for farming. In the end, very little of the vast public lands were acquired by individuals for farming. The great majority of the lands were bought up by large mining and lumber companies, who paid individuals the $1.25 to $2.50 down payment per acre required to take full possession of the land immediately.

Most of the black settlements that were established in the mid- to late 1870s were a modest variation on this theme. Colonization or real estate companies were formed to buy up land and have it plotted, and then settlers were urged to purchase it from those companies. The majority of black would-be homesteaders set their hopes on Kansas.

Part of the territories obtained by the United States from France in the Louisiana Purchase of 1803, Kansas remained a territory until the mid-1850s, when its residents sought admission to the Union. By that time, the issue of slavery had come to dominate the politics of the country, and admission of new states depended greatly on whether or not they were to be free states or slave states.

In 1854, in the hope of speeding the creation of new states in the territories of the Louisiana Purchase, Democratic Senator Stephen A. Douglas of Illinois introduced a Kansas-Nebraska Bill to Congress. The bill provided that the future of slavery in each individual territory or state be decided by its people. The bill passed both houses of Congress and was signed into law by President Franklin Pierce.

Antislavery forces were furious, for they believed that the bill authorized the extension of slavery into the West and would turn it into a land of masters and slaves. Equally angry were those whites who believed

Thousands of Missouri voters were ferried across the Missouri River to the Kansas shore to cast their votes, resulting in four times as many votes cast as there were voters in the territory!

In looking at this randomly armed raggle-taggle group en route to invade Kansas, one can see where the term "border ruffians" came from.

that the West should be kept free for white settlement alone. A resolution adopted at a free-soil meeting in Pittsburgh, Pennsylvania, in 1854, declared: "If the Douglas Nebraska bill should ever go into peaceful operation, which we doubt, it would completely Africanize the heart of the North American continent and divide the Free States of the Atlantic from the Free States of the Pacific by colonies of African boundmen and thereby exclude the free white race of the North from lands purchased by the whole nation from France. . . ."[17]

That resolution would prove to be prophetic in two ways. First, the free-soilers doubted that the Kansas-Nebraska Act could be put into peaceful operation, and they were right. The Act ignited a virtual civil war in Kansas. Farmers along the upper Mississippi Valley were opposed to the opening of any new lands to slavery and united to form the Republican Party. The New England Emigrant Aid Society pledged to send 20,000 antislavery settlers into Kansas. On election day 1855, 5,000 heavily armed men from Missouri took over voting booths and cast four times as many votes as there were voters in the territory. The governor of Kansas, Andrew H. Reeder, fled for his life, disguised as a peddler. The newly elected proslavery government of Kansas quickly took steps to wipe out all opposition to slavery in the territory. In response, Frederick Douglass—a former slave and prominent abolitionist—proposed to send into Kansas one thousand black families "as a wall of living fire to guard it."[18]

John Brown, an abolitionist who believed he had a divine mission to end slavery, raised an army of antislavery men in Ohio and set off for Kansas. While they were en route in the spring of 1856, 800 "Border Ruffians" from Missouri attacked and burned Lawrence, Kansas, a center of free-state forces. Brown and his men arrived too late to save Lawrence, but they retaliated by executing five proslavery men. Then 150 Border Ruffians attacked Brown's camp at Osawatomie. Undeterred, John Brown began to make plans to seize the federal arsenal at Harper's Ferry, Virginia, and to use the guns and ammunition stored there to free the local slaves. Brown and his forces raided the arsenal in the fall of 1859, but they were put down by federal troops and Brown was hanged.

In 1860, the Kansas Territory had a population of 625 free blacks and two slaves. Ten years later, the black population was 17,108. Most lived in eastern Kansas, near the Missouri River, where they lived and worked in towns or on small farms. They had arrived as individual families or in small groups—a slow, easily absorbed trickle. They were similar in every way but their color to other immigrants to the state and represented less than 5 percent of the population. But as Reconstruction wound down, more and more blacks looked to Kansas as a place where they could enjoy freedom and use their labor to benefit themselves rather than white landowners.

While Kansas had played a significant role in the events leading up to the Civil War, it had been largely unaffected by the war itself, which had been waged primarily in the South. In the postwar period, Kansas was booming. Railroads were being built, and new towns were springing up along their routes. Farming and cattle raising were a significant part of the state's economy, and "cow towns" like Dodge City and Abilene were established to care for the herds of longhorns being driven up from Texas to be shipped to the growing eastern cities. State officials and railroad builders were eager for more settlement in Kansas, and they encouraged anyone, black or white, to come.

Nicodemus, located in Graham County, Kansas, was the most prominent of the black colonies established in that state in the late Reconstruction era. It was located not far from Hill City, which had been laid out in the fall of 1876 by a white Indiana preacher named W. R. Hill. Hill sought additional people to settle in his area and encouraged black settlers, charging a $5 locating fee for each family, $2 of which he used to pay the government as a filing fee. A group of blacks from Kentucky who had made their way to Topeka seeking western lands provided the first population. They formed the Nicodemus Colony, and saw to the area's plotting as a government townsite on June 8, 1877.

Although some believe the colony's name had biblical origins, more likely it was named for a slave who, according to legend, foretold the Civil War. A song about him went as follows:

Nicodemus was a slave of African birth;
And was bought for a bag full of gold;
He was reckoned a part of the salt of the earth;
But he died years ago, very old.

This photo taken in Nicodemus, Kansas, around 1885 looks like it was taken straight from a Western movie set — except all of the town's residents are black.

Nicodemus was a prophet, at least he was as wise,
For he told of the battles to come;
How we trembled with fear, when he rolled up his eyes,
And we heeded the shake of his thumb.

Chorus:
Good time coming, good time coming,
Long, long time on the way;
Run and tell Elija to hurry up Pomp,
To meet us under the cottonwood tree,
In the Great Solomon Valley
At the first break of day.

On July 2, the Reverend S. P. Roundtree, secretary of the colony, issued the following circular, to be distributed by hand and published in newspapers, urging settlers to come.

To the Colored Citizens of the United States
Nicodemus, Graham Co., Kan., July 2d. 1877.

We, the Nicodemus Town Company of Graham County, Kan., are now in possession of our lands and the Town Site of Nicodemus, which is beautifully located on the N.W. quarter of Section 1, Town 8, Range 21, in Graham Co., Kansas, in the great Solomon Valley, 240 miles west of Topeka, and we are proud to say it is the finest country we ever saw. The soil is of a rich, black, sandy loam. The country is rather rolling, and looks most pleasing to the human eye. The south fork of the Solomon river flows through Graham County, nearly directly east and west and has an abundance of excellent water abounding throughout the Valley. There is an abundance of fine Magnesian stone for building purposes, which is much easier handled than the rough sand or hard stone. There is also some timber; plenty for fire use, while we have no fear but what we will find plenty of coal.

Now is your time to secure your home on Government Land in the Great Solomon Valley of Western Kansas.

Remember, we have secured the service of W. R. Hill, a man of energy and ability, to locate our Colony.

Not quite 90 days ago we secured our charter for locating the town site of Nicodemus. We then became an organized body, with only three dollars in the treasury and twelve members, but under the careful management of our offices, we have now nearly 300 good and reliable members, with several members permanently located on their claims—with plenty of provisions for the colony—while we are daily receiving letters from all parts of the country from parties desiring to locate in the great Solomon Valley of Western Kansas.

For Maps, Circulars, and Passenger rates, address our General Manager, W. R. HILL, North Topeka, Kansas, until August 1st, 1877, then at Hill City, Graham Co., via Trego.[19]

Many blacks responded to these advertisements. In Lexington, Kentucky, a group of blacks formed a "Colony" and resolved to consolidate itself with the Nicodemus Colony. A handbill advertising the plan was widely distributed:

ALL COLORED PEOPLE
THAT WANT TO
GO TO KANSAS
ON SEPTEMBER 5TH, 1877,
CAN DO SO FOR $5.00
IMMIGRATION

Whereas, We, the colored people of Lexington, Ky, knowing that there is an abundance of choice lands now belonging to the Government, have assembled ourselves together for the purpose of locating on said lands. Therefore,

Be It Resolved, That we do now organize ourselves into a Colony, as follows:—Any person wishing to become a member of this Colony can do so by paying the sum of one dollar ($1.00), and this money is to be paid by the first of September, 1877, in installments of twenty-five cents at a time, or otherwise as may be desired.

Resolved, That this Colony has agreed to consolidate itself with the Nicodemus Town, Solomon Valley, Graham County, Kansas, and can only do so by entering the vacant lands now in their midst, which costs $5.00.

Resolved, That this Colony shall consist of seven officers— President, Vice-President, Secretary, Treasurer, and three Trustees. President—M. M. Bell; Vice-President—Isaac Talbott; Secretary—W. J. Niles; Treasurer—Daniel Clarke; Trustees— Jerry Lee, William Jones, and Abner Webster.

Resolved, That this Colony shall have from one to two hundred militia, more or less, as the case may require, to keep peace and order, and any member failing to pay in his dues, as aforesaid, or failing to comply with the above rules in any particular, will not be recognized or protected by the Colony.[20]

By the following year, there were between 600 and 700 people in the town, having emigrated primarily from Kentucky, Tennessee, and Mississippi. W. H. Smith was the president of the colony. Z. T. Fletcher was the corresponding secretary. Fletcher also established the first school in his dugout shelter. Jenny Smith Fletcher, Z. T.'s wife, served as teacher, and average daily attendance at the school was about forty-five students. Fletcher also served as the first postmaster, operating from a dugout shelter where the mail was kept in a tea chest with a partition in it. For the first two years of operation, only two newspapers were regularly received at the Nicodemus Post Office. Once a week, W. H. Smith, president of the Nicodemus Colony, walked to the town of Ellis to collect the mail for Nicodemus and then walked back to Nicodemus with it.

Life on the Kansas prairie was hard. The major fact of life there was distance. The nearest trading points were often many miles away, and it was not economical for a single family to travel those distances for supplies. Townspeople would usually band together to finance an ox-drawn wagon to go to one of those trading points, and purchase their supplies by the wagon-load. A round-trip often took ten days to two weeks.

The hard Kansas soil was not easy to till, and an ox or mule team was essential for cultivating more than a few acres. Some corn could be raised, but the problem then was how to prepare it for food. The nearest mill was often many miles away, and settlers had to make do with drying it themselves and then breaking it up between two rocks to make hominy. Tea and coffee were great luxuries, and often chicory was used as a substitute. Before wells were dug, settlers relied on local streams for their drinking water, with the result that every year several people became ill.

The primary source of wood was the cottonwood tree, which was snarly in texture and difficult to split. That made building houses difficult, and most settlers didn't even bother trying to fence in their land.

Prairie fires were common, and with few roads to stop their progress they would sweep across the land, roaring over the tall grass. Drought was also common, forcing farmers to watch their fields and crops dry up.

When the first settlers arrived in Nicodemus, they did as American prairie settlers had always done before them—they constructed dugout shelters. On the flat Kansas prairie, dugouts were generally holes in the ground, the walls reinforced with wooden boards, their roofs made of grass and branches. Whenever possible, people set their shelters into a hillside. Another type of shelter, called a soddie, was made of blocks of earth set one upon the other like bricks. The earth provided warmth as well as protection from wind and rain. It was essential to build such shelters before winter came, because Kansas winters could be mean. As soon as they could, the settlers constructed stone houses, since there was not enough wood for home construction.

Among the early settlers were the Muldies, who had set out from Kentucky for Nicodemus in 1878. Originally a family of five, the wife died along the way, and Ed Muldie, a carpenter, and his three sons had gone on without her.

That first winter was hard for the people of Nicodemus. They had not had time to plant crops, and so their food supplies were low. Fortunately, local Osage Indians provided them with deer meat, dried fish, and dried beans, and they managed to survive.

By the time spring arrived, Ed Muldie had decided that the Kansas prairie was too flat for him. He wanted to go farther west in search of land. Leaving his three sons behind, where they stayed with friends, he set off on his search. The boys managed to fend for themselves, hunting and fishing for food. Three months went by with no word from their father. Then, at last, the post rider came with a letter from Ed Muldie. He had found free land near Solomon City, the letter said, and the boys were to join him. He enclosed a map showing where they were and where he was, 150 miles (241 kilometers) away, and how to get to him. They boys walked across the prairie, building a fire at night and occasionally shooting a gun to keep the coyotes, wolves, and panthers away. For twenty-two days they followed the Solomon River, until at last they were reunited with their father.

Free-born black northerners also heeded the possibilities of profit and living free on the American frontier. Among them was Edwin P. McCabe, born free in Troy, New York, in 1850. The eldest of three children in a poor family that moved frequently in search of work, McCabe lived and attended school in Massachusetts, Rhode Island, and Maine as a child. After his father died, McCabe was forced to discontinue his schooling in order to take a job and support his mother, sister, and brother. The family eventually moved to New York City, where McCabe found a job on Wall Street as a messenger. A light-complected man with an aquiline nose, piercing dark eyes, and a modest handle-bar mustache, McCabe was determined to succeed in life. At some point, he decided that his best opportunities lay in the West. After spending some time in Chicago, McCabe arrived in Kansas in 1874 and soon became involved in real estate and politics. Recognizing that blacks could best control their own lives if they could gain political control, he decided to encourage black migration to Kansas.

Even Henry Adams eventually came to see Kansas as the best place for his people. He had fervently hoped that the continued existence of some heavily Republican parishes in Louisiana would somehow hold the line against the Democrats in the election of 1878. He worked hard to get out the vote in those areas. But whites were just as determined to

76

At first glance, this photograph could be of slaves on a Southern plantation, but a careful look at the ground and building construction indicates that it is not the South at all. This family is in Kansas, eking out a hard living from the land.

Edwin McCabe headed to Kansas to escape the poverty of his Northern childhood— and that he did. He achieved success in politics and real estate and became a leader in the movements to migrate to Kansas and Oklahoma.

intimidate blacks from voting—by killing, beating, and whatever other means were necessary. If anything, white actions surrounding the election were more outrageous than ever, and at the behest of Republicans, a grand jury was convened in New Orleans to investigate the outrages. Henry Adams went to New Orleans to testify. In so doing, he effectively exiled himself, for several men had been killed en route to New Orleans, and anyone who testified and then tried to return home would be in danger. His mother had died in De Soto Parish shortly before he had left for New Orleans, and he was never to return home.

Adams remained in New Orleans, working from time to time at various jobs found for him by the remaining Republican senators. Unforeseen circumstances prevented him from even traveling around the environs of New Orleans to urge blacks to vote—and to vote Republican. An epidemic of yellow fever struck the towns along the Mississippi in the summer of 1878. It was particularly severe in Louisiana, and many towns were quarantined, making communication and travel difficult. Adams fell from the roof of a new Baptist Church he was helping to build and was forced to spend two months recovering. By the time he had recuperated, he found, to his great surprise, that the movement to emigrate to Kansas had gained great momentum. After the Democrats gained control of Louisiana politics in the election of 1878, while Adams's ultimate goal remained settlement in Liberia, he turned his attention to aiding the Kansas Exodus movement in any way he could.

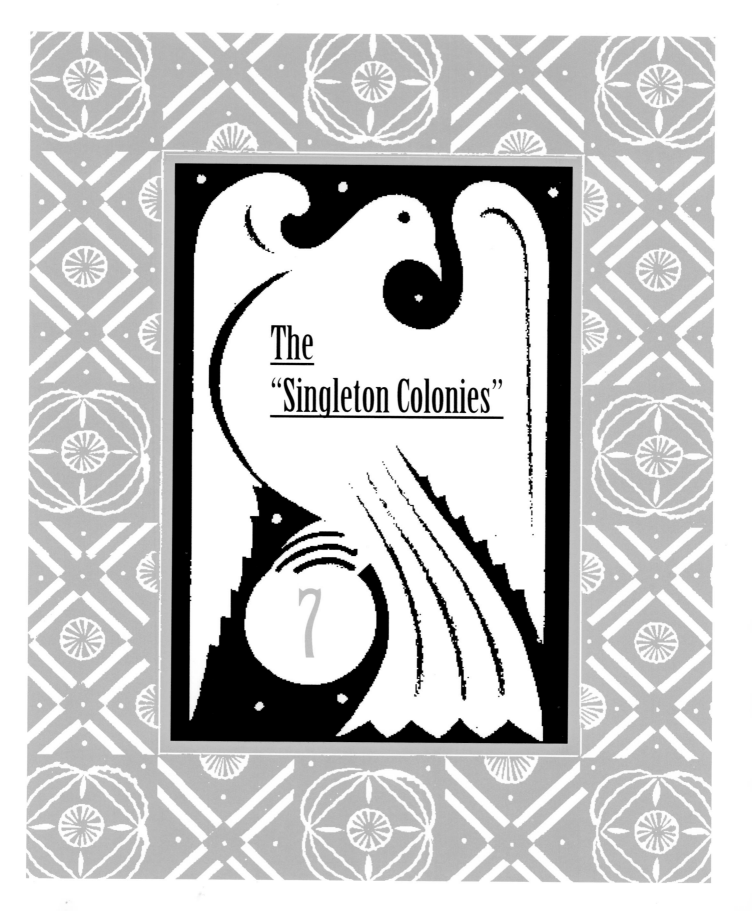

The
"Singleton Colonies"

7

Blacks were behaving like white Americans who had sought a better life on their own land.

In September 1874, Benjamin
Singleton and other black citizens of Nashville
who shared his views—including Elias Polk,
Robert Knowles, Randall Brown, Henry Carter,
and Daniel Wadkins—incorporated the
Edgefield Real Estate Association, with offices at
No. 5 Front Street, to purchase large tracts of
land in the frontier areas of Tennessee for home-
steading. The association held a convention in
May 1875 to discuss the question of migration.
As the site for the meeting, they chose Liberty
Hall, 44 Cedar Street, which had been built in
1872 by Nashville's first black bank, the
Freedmen's Savings and Trust Company.

Delegates to the convention charged that
they were not paid enough for their labor, and
when they were paid, they were paid late. They
complained that they were crowded into segre-

gated neighborhoods and denied even the most basic rights of citizenship. They voted to establish a Board of Emigration Commissioners and to send agents throughout Tennessee to inform potential migrants of the board's existence. Considered prime target areas were inhabitants of the large federal contraband camps that had been set up during the Civil War for escaped slaves and that after the war had continued to function as refugee camps for freedpeople who had nowhere to go. The delegates also voted to send representatives to Kansas to explore prospective areas for settlement in that state. In the meantime, delegates went back home and formed local emigration societies. The society in Nashville was called the Colored People's Cooperative Emigration Club and was formed "to improve the moral, intellectual, social, and material interests of the colored people."

The delegation to Kansas, headed by one H. A. Napier, returned to Nashville and reported their findings at an August 14 meeting. Napier reported that they had visited the region around the Great Bend of the Arkansas River and that the soil was good. But he also informed his listeners that the lack of timber, grasshopper plagues, and severe winter winds were hardly ideal conditions. He expressed concern over the cost of migrating to the region. By Napier's calculations, a migrant would have to save at least one thousand dollars to pay for transportation and provisions, a team of mules, a pair of plows, tools, lumber, tools for digging a well, and other expenses. One thousand dollars was a huge amount for blacks to save at that time, and Napier's report put a considerable damper on the spirits of the would-be emigrants at the meeting.

In August 1876, Singleton and an associate, W. A. Sizemore, wrote to Kansas Governor Thomas A. Osborn, informing him that many blacks in Tennessee wanted to relocate to Kansas but lacked the necessary funds to do so. The letter requested state government assistance in financing between fifty and one hundred families who wanted to take up farming in Kansas. The writers also assured Osborn that after a few years of hard work, the migrants would be able to repay the state. Although no state aid for the would-be migrants was forthcoming, Singleton and his associates apparently received assurances from Kansas state officials that black Tennesseeans were welcome.

The Edgefield Real Estate Association sent representatives to hold rallies in local black communities and raised funds by charging a nickel for admission to fundraising parties. They prepared posters announcing plans to emigrate to Kansas and also published newspapers to announce their emigration plans. In so doing, they were behaving much like white Americans who had sought and continued to seek a better life on their own land on the American frontier.

In early 1877, Singleton and his associate, Sumner county preacher Columbus M. Johnson, traveled to Kansas and established the Singleton Colony near Baxter Springs in Cherokee County, Kansas. Prior to the Civil War, the land that became Cherokee County had been part of the Cherokee and Quapaw Indian Reservations. Treaties signed in 1866 and 1867 between the two tribes and the federal government provided for the tribes to cede the land to the government, which in turn would sell the land and use the profits for the benefit of the tribal people. According to Benjamin Singleton, the price set for the land was too high at first, and after the government had trouble selling it, the price was reduced to $1.25 per acre.[21] This price Singleton and his emigrants could afford, usually with a down payment of one-sixth that sum in cash, and the remainder in six installments at 6 percent interest.

Singleton promoted the colony through advertisements such as one dated March 19, 1877:

> *Friends and Fellow Citizens,* —
> Having been to Kansas on a tour of inspection and examined the various inducements to emigration to that state, I feel it my duty to give all the information in my power to our poor down-trod-den race of Tennessee, in regard to the many advantages of Kansas. During my visit . . . [I] saw some excellent selections of land and plenty of fine water, with a healthy climate. There is abundant room for all good citizens, and no room for loafers or bummers. We want all good people there, who are willing to live by the sweat of their brow. Don't be misled by the false statements of adventurers and selfish speculators, for it is a fearful thing to fall into the hands of those traders.

All Colored People

THAT WANT TO

GO TO KANSAS,

On September 5th, 1877,

Can do so for $5.00

IMMIGRATION.

WHEREAS, We, the colored people of Lexington, Ky,. knowing that there is an abundance of choice lands now belonging to the Government, have assembled ourselves together for the purpose of locating on said lands. Therefore,

BE IT RESOLVED, That we do now organize ourselves into a Colony, as follows:— Any person wishing to become a member of this Colony can do so by paying the sum of one dollar ($1.00), and this money is to be paid by the first of September, 1877, in instalments of twenty-five cents at a time, or otherwise as may be desired.

RESOLVED. That this Colony has agreed to consolidate itself with the Nicodemus Towns, Solomon Valley, Graham County, Kansas, and can only do so by entering the vacant lands now in their midst, which costs $5.00.

RESOLVED, That this Colony shall consist of seven officers—President, Vice-President, Secretary, Treasurer, and three Trustees. President—M. M. Bell; Vice-President —Isaac Talbott; Secretary—W. J. Niles; Treasurer—Daniel Clarke; Trustees—Jerry Lee, William Jones, and Abner Webster.

RESOLVED, That this Colony shall have from one to two hundred militia, more or less, as the case may require, to keep peace and order, and any member failing to pay in his dues, as aforesaid, or failing to comply with the above rules in any particular, will not be recognized or protected by the Colony.

Singleton and his group used all of the capitalist resources available to them, including rallies, advertising, and membership on the installment plan!

84

Benjamin Singleton, the father of the Kansas emigration from Tennessee, the President of the Singleton Colony, is now laboring for the benefit of the down-trodden children of his race, to save them from poverty and degradation, crime and the prison; and all this free of charge.[22]

Exactly how Singleton could offer to transport emigrants to Kansas and settle them there free of charge he did not explain. But he later testified before Congress that he had "carried some people in there that when they got there they didn't have fifty cents left."[23]

According to a report in the August 9, 1877, issue of the Columbus *Republican Courier*, "The Singleton Colony, which is located on the Gulf road four miles this side of Baxter is rapidly filling up and we are informed that they intend in the course of a few weeks of laying out a town, have a post-office, newspaper and all the parapharnalia [*sic*] of an enterprising town." The report continued, stating that more than two thousand blacks had attended an emancipation meeting at Baxter Springs that summer and that a Mr. Stevenson, a traveling agent of the "Singleton colored colony," was on his way to Nashville for "a fresh supply of colored people."[24]

The Singleton colony in Baxter Springs never really got off the ground, however. A variety of problems beset the emigrants, the most serious being the lack of jobs. Unskilled and day labor opportunities were few, and without the chance to earn money, the migrants had great difficulty caring for themselves and their families. In March 1878, Kansas Governor George T. Anthony received a petition signed by more than 120 Cherokee County blacks asking for state aid to relieve their "want and suffering." By 1878, Singleton considered the Cherokee County colony so poorly managed that he withdrew his support and directed his attention to establishing a colony in another part of Kansas. The planned black town in Cherokee County never materialized.[25]

In the spring of 1878, Singleton established a colony at Dunlap in Morris County, Kansas, where affordable land was available under the 1862 Homestead Act. From 1846 to 1872, the land had been part of the

Kansa Indian Reservation. In 1872, after officials removed the Kansa Indians to Oklahoma, the government sold the land to any interested buyers. In 1874, Joseph Dunlap, who had been a trader to the Kansa Indians, laid out the town that bore his name.

By the time Benjamin Singleton scouted the area, most of the land in the Neosho River and creek valleys had already been settled, as were some of the uplands. No large block of land was available, so he created four upland settlements and one in the town of Dunlap itself, on the north side of the railroad tracks that extended from the valley floor northeast into the rocky uplands. Although the uplands were not prime farmland, Singleton considered them sufficient. At the time, the area was getting enough rainfall.

Perhaps to avoid what had happened to the Cherokee County colony, Singleton, W. A. Sizemore, and Alonzo DeFrantz all lived in the Dunlap colony from the middle of 1879 to the early part of 1880. They personally helped 200 emigrants from Tennessee move to the colony and to select and make down payments on farms that ranged in size from 40 to 80 acres (16 to 32 hectares).

Soon after they arrived in Dunlap, the new black residents began to celebrate Emancipation Day, an event that drew hundreds and sometimes thousands of people, black and white, including locals and their relatives, former residents, and local and state officials. The Dunlap blacks were becoming a real community. They had no idea that an influx of destitute emigrants would soon descend upon them.

The
Exodusters of 1879

8

Many of the migrants left home with little but the clothes on their backs.

Black out-migration from the South had thus far proceeded in a fairly orderly fashion. Beginning in 1877–1878, simmering unrest, continued white violence, and frightening political events combined to produce a frantic escape from the South by desperate freedpeople.

The most potent stimulus to flight was the end of Reconstruction and the withdrawal of the last federal troops from the former Confederate states. Southern blacks felt abandoned to "the wrath of their former masters," as Frederick Douglass put it. Most were deeply religious, and they could not believe that God would forsake them in this way after their hopes had been raised by the promises of Emancipation and by the Constitutional amendments that appeared to guarantee their social and political equality.

Some southern freedmen read or heard about the many editorials in black newspapers that urged them to leave the South and show southern landowners how much they needed black labor. An editorial in the July 26, 1878, issue of the black Baltimore newspaper, *The American Citizen*, is typical:

> . . . For colored men to stay in the rebel-ridden South and be treated like brutes is a disgrace to themselves and to the race to which they belong. The only way then that lies open to our people is to leave the South and come to the West. While we don't favor the colony idea very much, believing that the best course is to get as near other people as you can, yet, we would prefer that to being cheated and abused by the whites. When the South begins to lose her laborers in great numbers, then she will begin to see the folly of her course towards them, and her own necessities will force her to change her policies. . . .[26]

The black press also carried many advertisements for emigration placed by such men as Benjamin "Pap" Singleton, and there were a variety of posters, handbills, and other bits of advertising circulating in the South. Some carried glowing messages—and false promises—of free land and the ability to buy farm tools, provisions, and seeds on ten years' credit.

One intriguing circular writer, who went by the name of Lycurgus P. Jones (probably a pseudonym), warned his readers not to show the handbill to anyone but black people, thus ensuring that whites would make every effort to get at it. A New Orleans newspaper published one such Jones circular:

> (STRICTLY PRIVATE)
> ATTENTION COLORED MEN!
> OFFICE OF THE COLORED COLONIZATION SOCIETY
> TOPEKA, KANSAS
>
> Your brethren and friends throughout the North have observed with painful solicitude the outrages heaped upon you by your

rebel Masters, and are doing all they can to alleviate your miseries and provide for your future happiness and prosperity. President Hayes, by his iniquitous Southern policy, has deserted you, while the Democrats who now have control of Congress, will seek to enslave you if you remain in the South, and to protect you from their designs, the Colonization Society has been organized by the Government to provide land by each of a family, which will be given in bodies of one hundred and sixty acres gratuitously. This land is located in the best portion of Kansas, in close proximity to Topeka and is very productive. Here there are no class distinctions in society; all are on equality. Leave the land of oppression and come to free Kansas.

Lycurgus P. Jones, President[27]

Other handbills sought to appeal to those who could not read by depicting the productivity of the western soil and the success of those who went there: huge potatoes, apples, peaches, and ears of corn; black men riding in carriages wearing handsome suits and fingering large gold watch chains. Chromolithographs—colored engravings showing lovely homes and charming family scenes—spoke to the yearnings of the freedpeople to live in comfort and harmony.

Such advertisements fed the desperate dreams of southern blacks, and by the late winter of 1878–1879, hundreds had set off in search of their dream. Within weeks, the hundreds had become thousands—a massive, unplanned, unorganized movement the likes of which the country had never before seen.

Some who joined the movement had a little education and savings, had planned ahead and realized they faced considerable hardship wherever they went—at least until they established themselves. But the majority were poor, illiterate people with little or no money, who had not planned beyond getting away from white violence and grinding poverty, who were not so much going to a new place as leaving an old place, and who blindly trusted in Providence. They came to be called Exodusters.

Traveling by land and by water, the mass exodus to Kansas had begun…

The Exodusters regarded St. Louis, Missouri, as the gateway to the Promised Land. Getting to St. Louis meant that they had escaped from bondage. The Lord would take care of them after that. But just getting to St. Louis was difficult.

As determined as the Exodusters were to go to St. Louis, whites were equally determined to keep them at work in the fields. White employers had would-be migrants arrested for breach of contract—for not remaining at work under the conditions of labor contracts they had signed. Some whites, already accustomed to using violence and intimidation against blacks, formed themselves into vigilante mobs to accost groups of Exodusters on the roads and turn them back by any means necessary.

Many of the migrants left home with little but the clothes on their backs and a bundle of food and other belongings. They had to depend on the kindness of strangers they encountered along the way to provide them with food and shelter. Their meager supplies of food were soon exhausted, and they slept in fields and woods at night, away from main roads that might harbor vigilante groups looking to stop them.

If they were fortunate enough to reach the river, they then had to wait on its banks and levees until a steamboat came along whose captain was willing to take them north. Many were unaware that securing steamboat passage was not that simple. Rumors had taken hold that railroad companies seeking to encourage emigration to areas planned as depots in the West would pay the passage of anyone willing to go to those areas. Although the railroad companies tried to quell those rumors, publishing notices in newspapers that they would pay the passage only of people who had bought land from them, the majority of Exodusters never saw those notices. In an attempt to quell the exodus, the St. Louis packets briefly refused to take them on.

Still, they remained on the river banks in the hope that Divine Providence would rescue them. There, they were sometimes visited by black agents employed by planters and businessmen to persuade them to sign new labor contracts or simply to return to where they had come from. Some Exodusters gave up and did as they were asked. But most remained on the levees.

Exodusters, with all of their possessions in tow, sit on the banks of the Mississippi in the hope of finding room on a passing steamboat to take them North.

An observer wrote in the *Cincinnati Commercial*:

The encampments all had hailing-signals up for the north-bound steamboats, and when these wildly, frantically waved signals were cruelly ignored while the boat proceeded complacently on its way, I saw colored men and women cast themselves to the ground in despair, and heard them groan and shout their lamentations.

What is to become of these wretched people God only knows. Here were nearly half a thousand, refused, scattered along the banks of the mighty Mississippi, without shelter, without food, with no hope of escaping from their present surrounding, and hardly a chance of returning whence they came.[28]

Almost immediately, groups in Kansas and elsewhere who were sympathetic to the Exodusters filed lawsuits against the steamship companies to force them to carry the pilgrims north. Thomas H. Conway, who had been a commissioner of the Freedmen's Bureau and the Louisiana State commissioner of education until 1872, was appalled at the plight of the Exodusters. While supporting lawsuits brought against the steamship companies for discrimination, he also came up with a scheme to charter special transportation to convey the refugees up the river. Under threat of both lawsuits and the charter transportation scheme, the Anchor Steamship Line, the main riverboat line, finally agreed to start carrying the Exodusters to St. Louis again. The refusal to carry the refugees had lasted only about a month, but it effectively killed the momentum of the Exoduster movement. Migrants continued to travel north, but in nowhere near the great numbers of earlier in the spring.

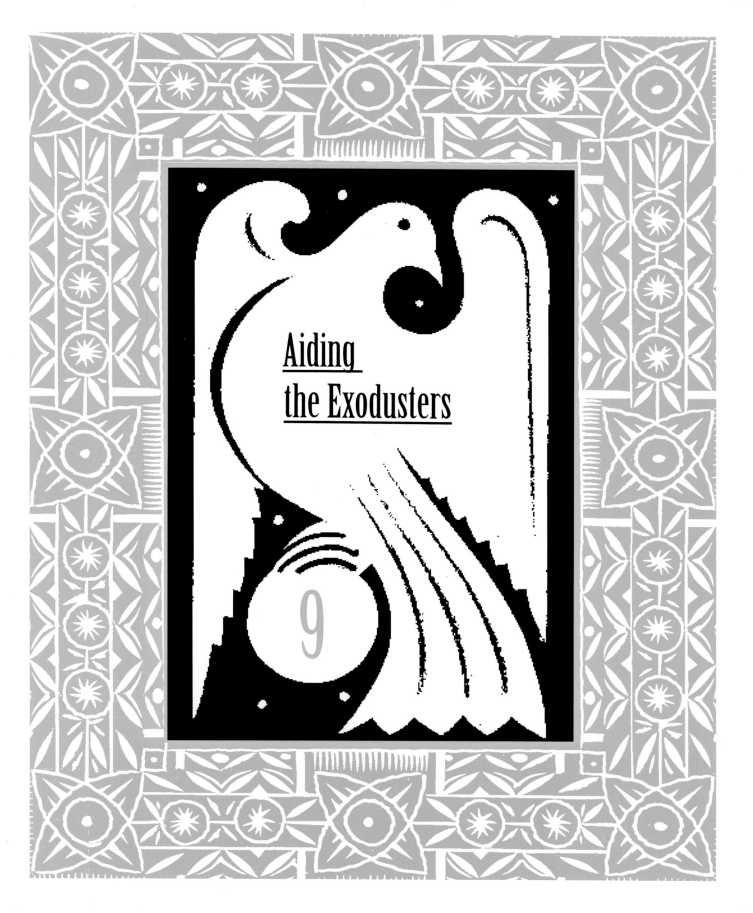

Aiding
the Exodusters

9

As the sheer size
of the black exodus
became apparent, efforts
to aid the immigrants
were organized.

St. Louis was unprepared to be the gateway to the Promised Land for the black would-be homesteaders who began to arrive in the late winter of 1879. Charleton H. Tandy, a black politician in St. Louis, was the first to take measures of relief for the emigrants. He sought help from the Mullanphy Emigrant Relief Board, which was administered by the city of St. Louis and which had been set up to aid migrants and immigrants on their way to the West. But the board refused Tandy's initial plea. Only after repeated efforts did Tandy manage to secure the sum of $100 for the relief of the black refugees. This was hardly enough for the stream of hungry and impoverished people who daily entered the city—and it was $200 less than the board had appropriated for the relief of white families in the same circumstances.[29]

Mayor Henry Overstolz of St. Louis sought to prevent more Exodusters from arriving. He sent an official message to local authorities along the Mississippi in an attempt to discourage the Exodusters. He also tried to enforce a local ban on bringing indigents into the city. The city's Board of Health refused to house the Exodusters in its quarantine station. The only efforts whites in St. Louis made on behalf of the Exodusters was to dispense with them as quickly as possible. The Anchor Steamship Line, based in St. Louis, offered free passage back to the South for all Exodusters, an offer that only a handful of migrants accepted.

It was clear to the black people of St. Louis that they would have to take care of their own, and they rose to the task, taking emigrant families into their homes and donating money to the relief cause. Soon, a group of St. Louis blacks had formed the Colored Relief Board and asked each black organization in the city to contribute five dollars to the Exodusters' relief, an initiative that raised more than fifty dollars. Much of the money was used to pay passage for the emigrants to Kansas, for most of the Exodusters had made it to St. Louis on the little money they had and could not afford to go farther. To care for them until they could be sent west, black churches opened up their sanctuaries. In the period between about March 9 and March 21, some 1,400 Exodusters arrived in the city and were housed in three churches and in homes in St. Louis.

By the third week of April, the need to put the organization on a firmer footing led to the incorporation of the board as the Colored People's Board of Emigration of the City of St. Louis. That same month, the board sent two representatives to Kansas to look into the condition of the people it had sent there. Charleton Tandy made a fundraising trip to the East. In Washington, he met with local black leaders, and together they spoke before several aid meetings in the nation's capital and in New York City.

Also in mid-April, the Emigrant Aid Association was organized in Washington, D.C. It turned its sights on Kansas, the final destination of many of the Exodusters, and cooperated with the scattered and disorganized relief efforts in Topeka and elsewhere.

The black citizens of St. Louis welcomed
the early waves of emigrants, but soon the
numbers became overwhelming.

For many migrants, the last leg of their journey to Kansas was by steamboat up the Missouri River to the border between Missouri and Kansas. If they disembarked at Kansas City, Missouri, they faced a hostility similar to that in St. Louis. Kansas City residents did not want the Exodusters, and a local newspaper, the *Times*, went so far as to accuse St. Louis of dumping its "paupers and thieves" on Kansas City. A white resident of Wyandotte, Kansas, just across the river, seemed to agree with this notion when he commented that it looked like "all the alm houses of the Mississippi Valley had been searched to get them together."[30] But by contrast to Kansas City, Wyandotte residents made sincere efforts to help the newcomers, and word soon spread among the Exodusters that Wyandotte was by far the more hospitable port of debarkation. The small Kansas town of some five thousand residents opened its churches to provide shelter; volunteers nursed the sick and buried the dead; and contributions of money and food poured in. But as the steamships of the Anchor line—the *Joe Kinney*, the *Fanny Lewis*, the *Durfee*—kept coming, a rising sense of concern took hold. An influx that in early April 1878 numbered about six hundred, soon swelled to more than a thousand after the arrival of the *Durfee*, and by mid-month there were an estimated two thousand refugees in Wyandotte. One of the town's leaders remarked, "We shall certainly be swamped. We are not panic stricken, although the shrill whistle of every boat which comes causes us many anxious thoughts."[31]

A special committee of town leaders drafted an appeal for help that was sent to newspapers across the country. Addressed to "the generous citizens of the United States," it pleaded for help in the relief effort: "In the midst of this general suffering and great need for immediate aid we send this Macedonian cry for immediate assistance."[32]

When, by the third week of April, more steamboats had landed and word came that others were on the way, Wyandotte had had enough. Even its older black residents were turning against the Exodusters. Mayor Stockton of Wyandotte issued a proclamation, addressed to all steamboat lines and transportation companies, threatening legal action if they continued to bring destitute persons to his city. Two days later, when the *Durfee* arrived with another 240 Exodusters, an official delegation stood waiting on shore with the news that the captain could not unload his passengers at Wyandotte. Captain George Keith of the *Durfee* angrily objected, but to no avail; he then shoved off and deposited his cargo at Kansas City.

As the sheer size of the black exodus became apparent, efforts to aid the immigrants were organized. Blacks who had already arrived—and particularly those who had established settlements—were determined to help the people who had heeded the call of "Ho to Kansas!" By the third week of April, close associates of Benjamin "Pap" Singleton had come together to establish a relief organization, which soon joined forces with a second relief organization, the Freedmen's Aid Association, formed just one day later by whites. By contrast to St. Louis whites, who gave only grudging aid to the emigrants, whites in Topeka seemed to view the arrival of the Exodusters as the logical outcome of the events in Kansas that had figured so prominently in the years leading up to the Civil War.

In the two years of its operation, the Kansas Freedmen's Relief Association (KFRA) sought funds from across the nation as well as in England, and raised more than $90,000 in cash and supplies. It worked to find jobs for Exodusters in Kansas and in neighboring states, helped establish them in existing black colonies, and even started new colonies.

Early on, Benjamin Singleton's Dunlap colony formed its own branch of the KFRA, and in cooperation with the Presbyterian Church, played a major role in relocating Topeka refugees to the Dunlap area. The Presbyterian Synod of North America assigned the Reverend John M. Snodgrass as a missionary to the blacks of Dunlap, and Snodgrass was instrumental in the church's building a literary and business academy there. Opened in 1880, it was chartered as The Freedmen's Academy of Kansas with the mission "to educate the colored youth for teaching, for business management, for mechanical industries, for an honorable social life; and to encourage the settlement of destitute colored families of the cities on cheap lands in the country." The church assigned two black teachers to the school, Andrew Atchison as principal and Maggie Watson as the primary school teacher.[33] The Dunlap, or Singleton, Colony later became an educational center for blacks in Kansas, with, in

addition to the Freedmen's Academy, two primary schools, and an industrial school sponsored by Quakers.

Among its relief efforts on behalf of the Exodusters, the Kansas Freedmen's Relief Association established colonies for the new arrivals. One was the Wabaunsee Colony, located about 50 miles (80 kilometers) west of Topeka in Wabaunsee County. Before the Civil War, citizens of Wabaunsee County, which had not been settled until 1854, had been active in the Underground Railroad. Two "stations" had existed, one at Mission Creek and one at the town of Wabaunsee. As many as eighteen escaped southern slaves were conducted first to Mission Creek, and from there, at night, to Wabaunsee, whereupon they were taken to Fremont County, Iowa. The KFRA purchased 1,280 acres (518 hectares) of land with a down payment and settled thirty-one families there, who had nineteen years to pay the balance due. The association built barracks to house the families temporarily until they could build their own homes. Isaiah Montgomery, a black Mississippi planter, bought some of the Wabaunsee Colony land for his own use, and while remaining on his Mississippi plantation, employed nine black families. By the end of 1880, the KFRA pronounced the Wabaunsee Colony self-sustaining.

Another colony established by the KFRA was located in Hodgeman County, about 25 miles (40 kilometers) north of Dodge City. The KFRA advertised the existence of the colony and urged blacks to settle there. One of their handbills read in part:

COME!

To the Colored People of the United States of America:

This is to lay before your minds a few sketches of what great advantages there are for the great mass of people of small means that are emigrating to the West to come and settle in the county of Hodgeman, in the State of Kansas—and more especially the Colored people, for they are the ones that want to find the best place for climate and for soil for the smallest capital. Hodgeman county is in Southwestern Kansas, on the line of the Atchison, Topeka & Santa Fe Railroad.

We, the undersigned, having examined the above county . . .[34]

Sometimes called Kinsley Colony, after the closest rail connection at Kinsley in Edwards County, the Hodgeman County settlement, originally numbering one hundred and seven people, was later reinforced by fifty more. Members of the colony soon concluded that they were too isolated and tried to start a town closer to Kinsley. They called their town Morton City and purchased some fifty homesteads. But the huge distances, the costs of transporting supplies, and the task of building a town while trying to farm the hard Kansas sod were too difficult.

Among the Kinsley Colony settlers was Lafayette Green, who owned a small piece of property in Kentucky but who had moved to Kansas with his wife seeking greater opportunity. The couple left their six children behind in Kentucky until that land was sold or they could make a proper home in Kansas. Green and his wife built a 14-by-14-foot (4-by-4-meter) dugout 5 feet (1.5 meters) underground and 2 feet (.6 meter) above, covered with pine boards that served as a roof. In the spring of 1879, he prepared 8 acres (3 hectares) for cultivation—six in wheat, two in corn, plus a small garden. He tried to dig a well but hit solid rock at 13 feet (4 meters) and had to travel a mile (1.6 kilometers) to get water. His wife became ill. Green feared leaving his Kansas claim, concerned that if he did not follow the homestead law, which provided that a homesteader must remain on his claim, he would lose his Kansas land. History has not recorded what happened to him.[35]

After erecting a frame building intended as a store, and a few sod huts, the settlers abandoned Morton City and dispersed.

Although such relief colonies helped the situation caused by the Exodusters of 1879, there was no way to create enough colonies for all the emigrants. Not only were time and money major factors, so was the new attitude among the state's residents. Kansans had not counted on the size of the exodus, and it was not long before a backlash occurred and concerns mounted about the growing blackness of the state. By 1880, the number of blacks in Kansas had jumped to 43,107, and although that number still represented less than 5 percent of the total population, it was too many for some whites. The exodus brought to the surface hidden hostilities toward blacks that might have remained submerged had black migration to the state continued in the orderly fashion of the pre-Exoduster years.

Nevertheless, Kansas remained for a time a true haven for blacks—a place where one could prosper and live in relative freedom. Once established in Kansas, Edwin P. McCabe, the New Yorker who had arrived in Kansas in 1874 by way of Chicago, found that he was courted by Republicans, who realized that the Exodusters who were arriving by the thousands in the state would vote for a black man. McCabe was only thirty-two years old when he was chosen as the Republican Party candidate for the office of state auditor. Of the four hundred delegates to the Republican nominating convention, only six were black, but McCabe was nominated by acclamation. One nominating speech called him "the recognized leader of his race in the west."[36] Republicans were in control in Kansas at the time, and having secured the party's nomination, McCabe easily won the nomination, the first black man to be elected to state office in the United States. Two years later, he was re-elected.

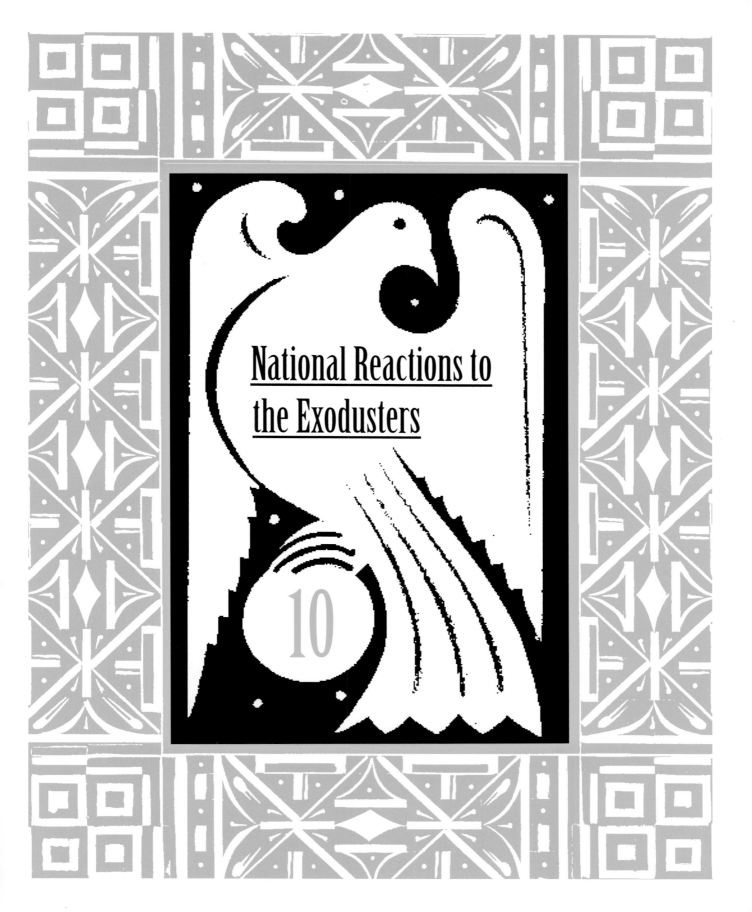

National Reactions to
the Exodusters

10

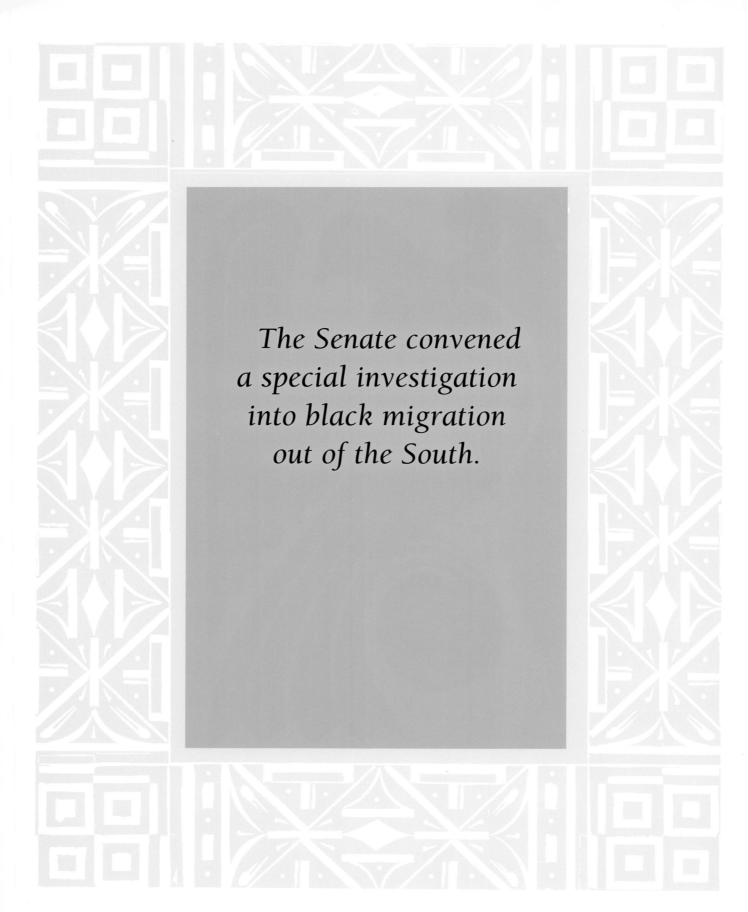

The Senate convened a special investigation into black migration out of the South.

Most important black leaders in the United States understood and supported the Exoduster movement. Sojourner Truth, whose accounts of slavery had made her one of the most popular speakers on the abolitionist lecture circuit before the Civil War, wrote a poem about the exodus that spoke to its biblical references: "The word it has been spoken; the message has been sent. The prison doors have opened, and out the prisoners went."[37]

But there were some who opposed the exodus. J. Milton Turner, former ambassador to Liberia, was one. Others were P. B. S. Pinchback, who had served as lieutenant governor of Louisiana during Reconstruction, and T. T. Allain, a member of the Louisiana House of Representatives. Frederick Douglass, the most well-known black leader who spoke out against

111

the exodus, expressed consternation over the movement. He had believed and promised for so long that all the southern slaves needed was to be free, after which they would become respectable and productive citizens, that he could not see the truth. He feared that the black exodus would "cast upon the people of Kansas and other Northern states a multitude of deluded, hungry, homeless, naked and destitute people." In a letter to the newspaper, *National Republican*, printed in the paper's May 5, 1879, issue, Douglass asserted that he was "opposed to this exodus" because "I see in it a tendency to convert colored laboring men into traveling camps." He argued that conditions in the South were steadily improving and predicted that "the colored man there will ultimately realize the fullest measure of liberty and equality."[38]

Blacks in the South were aghast that Douglass could write such blather. The South of which Frederick Douglass spoke existed only in his dreams. Where was the great leader's fabled compassion and intellectual grasp of complex situations? Northern blacks felt a sense of betrayal as well, and Douglass began to experience outright hostility from his people for the first time in his life.

"In all my forty years of thought and labor to promote the freedom and welfare of my race," he later wrote, "I never found myself more widely and painfully at variance with leading colored men of the country." Nevertheless, he continued to assert, "I never took a position in which I felt myself better fortified by reason and necessity."[39]

The American Social Science Association decided to take up the question of the structure of laboring classes in the South at its annual meeting at Saratoga Springs, New York, in September 1879. In particular, the officials of the association were interested in the black migration out of the South, and to argue the issue, they invited two black thinkers to present papers at the conference. Douglass was asked to speak in opposition to emigration. To speak for it, they invited Richard T. Greener.

Greener, the first black graduate of Harvard University, had taught at the University of South Carolina during Reconstruction. By 1877, he was teaching at Howard University, the black college in Washington, D.C., and had been one of the founders of the Emigrant Aid Association organized in the capital to help the Exodusters. Douglass, as a trustee of

Howard University, had already had disagreements with Greener, and he was concerned, and rightly so, that his appearance at the convention would be controversial. At first, he decided to attend. But he sent his paper ahead and planned to arrive just before the conference began, hoping to be greeted, as he told a friend, "in the spirit of social science and not in the spirit of controversy."[40] But in the end, he did not go, wiring the organizers of the conference to that effect just a day before it was scheduled to begin.

Without Frederick Douglass there in person to argue his case, there was no confrontation at the conference. His paper, read in his absence, began with statements of sympathy for the Exodusters. Rather than slaughter their oppressors "by fire and sword," as emancipated slaves had done in Haiti, American freed people had "adopted a simple, lawful and peaceable measure. It is emigration—the quiet withdrawal of his valuable bones and muscles from a condition of things which he considers no longer tolerable." But Douglass argued that the labor of freed people had built the South, and that the freed person "stands today the admitted author of whatever prosperity, beauty and civilization are now professed by the South. He is the arbiter of her destiny."[41]

Douglass eventually concluded that he had been wrong not to support the Exoduster movement. In March 1888, he visited South Carolina and Georgia and observed for himself the terrible plight of black sharecroppers. He later reported that he had "seen enough, heard enough, and learned enough. . . to make me welcome any movement which will take them [the sharecroppers] out of the wretched condition in which I now know them to be."[42]

The vast majority of southern whites either disdained the exodus as an insignificant movement, or made it their business to stop the drain of labor the exodus represented. But some actually welcomed the exodus, hailing it as a means of getting rid of poor workers. Their argument was that discontented blacks would not be productive, and so it was better for the South to be rid of them.

Those whites hoped that the places of the migrant blacks would be filled with immigrants from Europe or the Far East. This attitude was especially prevalent in Texas, which had attracted a sizeable number of German immigrants. That the Germans, just like the blacks, were more

Although the initial situation in Kansas had all of the problems of any unplanned mass immigration, those who stuck it out seemed to fare well. Compare this photo of a Kansas black family outside their modest but comfortable family residence with the conditions of slavery just thirty years before.

Look, too, at the portrait of the Albert Salisbury family, Kansas homesteaders in 1882. There seem to be three generations, all together—a virtual impossibility under their earlier life of slavery.

interested in owning and cultivating their own land than in working for white planters, seemed not to occur to them. Also, the South in general was not an attractive place for European immigrants, who tended to be more interested in entering trades than in cultivating land and who sought the public services, such as schools, that the immigrant-rich North offered, but which were woefully lacking in the South.

Other southern whites advocated importation of Chinese laborers, who had arrived in the United States in large numbers to work on construction of the transcontinental railroads. Some whites even made inquiries to the Chinese Six Companies in San Francisco, which controlled most of the Chinese laborers in the United States. But the Chinese Six Companies replied that they would not send Chinese laborers to the South on the terms offered—fifty cents a day without board.

In the end, the exodus did not prove to be a significant drain on the southern labor force, and talk of importing foreign immigrants subsided.

The tremendous influx of black southerners into the middle west caused great concern among representatives of those states in the federal government. Senator John J. Ingalls of Kansas and Representative James A. Garfield of Ohio both introduced bills that called for the appropriation of money to aid the refugees. But neither bill passed. Nor did Congress take any further action until a similar exodus, this time from North Carolina to Indiana, occurred. At that point, when the Mississippi-Louisiana-Kansas exodus was almost a year old, the Senate convened a special investigation into the causes and possible consequences of the black migration out of the South.

Ordinary Exodusters were called to testify before the Senate Select Committee Investigating the "Negro Exodus from the Southern States." So were leaders of the migration, including both Henry Adams and Benjamin "Pap" Singleton. Those who testified told of the hardships suffered by southern blacks, of bulldozing and Black Codes and white violence.

"How was it," a senator asked Henry Adams, "that there were five or six colored people to one white man, the white people could bulldoze the Negro and prevent him from voting?"

Adams replied, "The whites told all the colored men, 'If you don't vote our way you had better not go home for we are going to kill every damn nigger that votes the radical ticket today.' A great many colored men left the polls. Several white men had large revolvers and they told the colored men they had to vote their way or die. So all that voted, voted the Democratic ticket, but seventeen colored men who voted Republican. Of them who had any crops it was taken away from them, and a great many of them was run away."

"Why do not the colored people arm themselves?" Adams was asked. "Cannot they get arms?"

"They can buy arms if they have the money," Adams answered, "till the riot comes. If there is a riot started, [the whites] go down by fifties and hundreds in a gang to watch us to see whether the colored men are going to buy arms. At the time a riot is going on, the colored men cannot buy no ammunition.

"If the colored men are attacked, they call it a riot, because they are killing the colored men. You never hear of the colored man raising the riot, because he never gets the chance. If he shoots a white man they kill fifty colored men for the one white man that was shot." [43]

Henry Adams concluded, "In 1877, we lost all hopes. The whole South—every state in the South—had got into the hands of the very men that held us slaves." [44]

Singleton was asked why he had gone to Kansas and established colonies for freedmen.

Q. What was the cause of your going out, and in the first place how did you happen to go there, or to send these people there?
A. Well, my people, for the want of land—we needed land for our children—and their disadvantages—that caused my heart to grieve and sorrow; pity for my race, sir, that was coming down instead of going up—that caused me to go to work for them. I sent [representatives] out there [to Kansas] perhaps in '66—perhaps so; or in '65, any way—my memory don't recollect which; and they brought back tolerable favorable reports; then I jacked up three or four hundred [dollars], and went into Southern Kansas, and found it was a good country, and I thought Southern Kansas was congenial to our nature, sir; and I formed a colony

there, and bought about a thousands acres of ground—the colony did—my people.

Q. And they went upon it and settled there?

A. Yes, sir; they went and settled there.

Q. Were they men with some means or without means?

A. I never carried none there without means.

Q. They had some means to start with?

A. Yes; I prohibited my people leaving their country and going there without they had money—some money to start with and go on with a while.

In practically his next statement, Singleton contradicted himself somewhat when he said,

"I have carried some people in there that when they got there they didn't have fifty cents left, and now they have got in my colony—Singleton colony—a house, nice cabins, their milch cows, and pigs, and sheep, perhaps a span of horses, and trees before their yeards, and some three or four or ten acres broken up, and all of them has got little houses that I carried there. They didn't go under no relief assistance; they went on their own resources, and when they went in there first the country was not overrun with them; you see they could get good wages; the country was not overstocked with people; they went to work, and I never helped them as soon as I put them on the land."

Singleton claimed to have "fetched out 7,432 people." He also told the Senate committee about his divine inspiration to lead his people to Kansas: "Right emphatically, I tell you today, I woke up the millions right through me! The great God of glory has worked in me. I have had open air interviews with the living spirit of God for my people; and we are going to leave the South. We are going to leave it if there ain't an alteration and signs of change."[45]

"I am the whole cause of the Kansas immigration!" Singleton stated. "You take all that responsibility on yourself?" he was asked. "I do, and I can prove it; and I think I have done a good deal of good, and I feel relieved!" responded Singleton.[46]

Singleton's testimony that he was the father of the Exoduster movement led to the general public acceptance of his claim—even though he was merely one among many so-called leaders in what was essentially a leaderless movement.

Having heard testimony so extensive that it filled three volumes, the majority of the Senate committee came to the same opinion as they had held when they first convened: Democrats concluded that the South was a good place for blacks and that politically motivated Republican agitators were the cause of the unrest. According to this line of thinking, Republicans had concluded that black votes could no longer do any good in the South, where Democrats had reasserted dominance, and that the exodus movement was aimed at moving those voters to northern states in order to tip the balance of power to the Republicans. Life in the South for blacks was ". . . not only as good as could have been reasonably expected, but it is better than if large communities were transferred to a colder and more inhospitable climate, thrust into competition with a different system of labor, among strangers who are not accustomed to them, their ways, habits of thought and action, their idiosyncracies, and their feelings. . . ."[47]

But a minority report issued by Republican senators Henry Blair of New Hampshire and William Windom of Minnesota cited the testimony of Henry Adams and Benjamin Singleton as proof that "great causes must exist at the South to account for [the exodus]." Blair and Windom cited the majority report itself as proof that political, not human, considerations were at the forefront of the committee's investigation:

"In the presence of [the] most diabolic outrages clearly proven; in the face of the declaration of thousands of refugees that they had fled because of the insecurity of their lives and property at the South, and because the Democratic party of that section had, by means too shocking and shameful to relate, deprived them of their rights as American citizens; . . . in the face of all these facts the majority of the committee can see no cause for the exodus growing out of such wrongs, but endeavor to charge it to the Republicans of the North."[48]

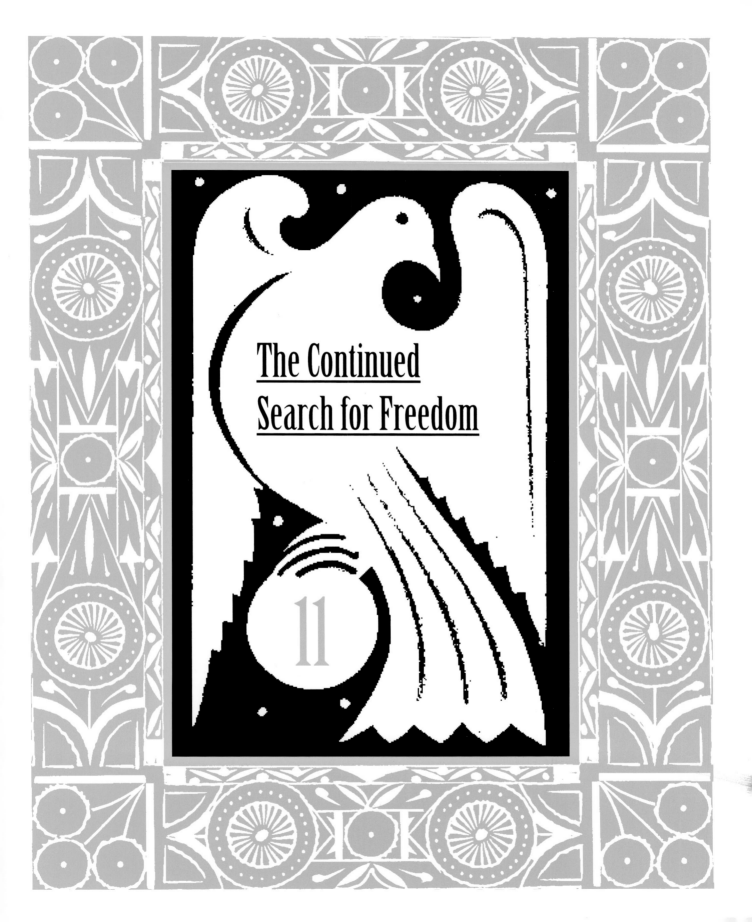

The Continued
Search for Freedom

11

*The Exodusters proved
that many blacks were
unwilling to accept economic
and social victimization.*

The eloquent testimony of Henry Adams before the United States Senate Committee on the Negro Exodus assured Adams's place in history, but it was also among the final records of Adams. He was last heard from in 1884, at which time he would have been only in his early fifties—still in his prime, unless illness or accident befell him.

Benjamin "Pap" Singleton lived to be celebrated as the "Moses of the Exodus" and the "Grand Old Man." He also lived to see his hopes for black freedom and prosperity in the West dashed. By 1881, he had, like Edwin McCabe before him, realized the possibilities for blacks in Kansas politics and had entered politics for the first time, organizing a political party called United Colored Links in a black section of Topeka, Kansas, called "Tennessee Town" because so many of its residents were from that

in particular, they appeared in black churches and public halls across the South and sent letters to newspapers, preachers, and schoolteachers urging all who had the courage to migrate to the West. Altogether, McCabe helped African Americans establish thirty all-black towns in Oklahoma. But in spite of his efforts, when Oklahoma was admitted to statehood in 1907, it entered the Union as a segregated state. Soon afterward, McCabe left Oklahoma for Chicago, where he died penniless in 1920.

Booker T. Washington, founder of Tuskegee University and one of the most influential black leaders of his time, compared the migration of southern blacks to Oklahoma around the turn of the century with the Kansas migration of twenty years earlier. In his book, *My Larger Education*, published in 1911, he stated that the Oklahoma migrants "came with a definite notion of where they were going; they brought a certain amount of capital with them, and had a pretty clear idea of what they would find and what they proposed to do when they reached their destination." For Washington, the difference between the two migrations indicated the extent to which the race had progressed.[50]

The idea of "repatriation to Africa" enjoyed a renaissance after Reconstruction ended. Several emigration societies were established, among them the Liberian Exodus Joint-Stock Steamship Company, founded in South Carolina, which in 1878 sent a party of 206 people out of Charleston harbor on the ship *Azor*, bound for Africa.[51] More such societies arose in the 1890s, but none succeeded in gaining the influence once held by the American Colonization Society.

The American Colonization Society remained in operation, but it enjoyed nowhere near the influence it had held in the past. In the last decade of the nineteenth century, Bishop Henry McNeal Turner, a leader of the African Methodist Episcopal Church, was an energetic public spokesman for emigration. He had traveled to Liberia and was excited about its promise. His letters about Liberia were published in church newspapers in 1891, and among those who responded to his call were black families who had tried and failed to find the freedom they sought in the West. While the populations of black towns in Mississippi, Arkansas, Kansas, and Oklahoma continued to grow, some families who had tried life in those towns made their way to New York City in hopes of securing passage to Liberia.

124

One contingent arrived from Arkansas, where they had formed local clubs to encourage emigration. But in New York City they found that the American Colonization Society did not have either the ships to carry them or the funds to pay their passage. The ACS had fallen on financial hardship, and even an administrative reorganization after 1892 failed to revive it. Most of the people who went to New York City in hopes of finding a way to get to Liberia became urban refugees, and eventually settled in the city or returned to the West.

Blacks who had settled in Kansas faced considerable discrimination from white Kansans. In September 1879, according to a report in the *Morris County Times*, blacks at a benefit barbecue for Exodusters were not permitted to join in a quadrille with the whites. The following March, the same newspaper reported, "There will be a meeting of colored citizens of Dunlap township to take into consideration a graveyard, as [there is] a public objection to colored people being buried where good Republicans are buried. . ."[52] Not long afterward, blacks established their own cemetery north of the white one. Separate schools and churches soon followed, and residential areas became segregated, with blacks to the north of the railroad tracks and whites to the south.

In some ways, racial discrimination was the least of the worries with which the blacks of Dunlap Colony had to contend. Climate and the nature of the soil in the uplands presented major difficulties. While the average rainfall was enough for crops, rains were highly erratic, and often came all at once or not at all. The thin soil of the uplands was prey to erosion, very rocky, almost timberless, and without ready access to water. Also, while a minimum of 160 acres (64 hectares), including both bottomlands and upland pastures, was needed for a succesful farm, the majority of black homesteads comprised only 40 to 80 acres (16 to 24 hectares).

Those who had the means soon switched from raising corn and hogs to raising cattle. The early 1880s were boom years for cattle raising in Dunlap and most other parts of the West; blacks who did not operate their own ranches found plentiful work as laborers on the ranches of others. In the fall of 1882, according to the *Topeka Daily Capital*, there were between 275 and 300 blacks families in Dunlap and vicinity. The "cattle bust" of 1887, followed by a nationwide economic depression beginning in 1889, had a severe impact on the fortunes of the Kansas farmers and ranchers.

The Freedmen's Academy closed in the early 1890s, and thus the state's blacks lost their opportunity for a free education, not to mention the economic assistance the academy's backers had provided. Between 1895 and 1905, the number of black families in the region declined steadily. By the time of the Great Depression, so few black families remained that the black schools were closed and the public schools were integrated. The last Emancipation Day celebration was held on September 22, 1931. Two black churches remained in operation until the early 1950s, but in the last years of their existence both were supported by only a few families. By 1991, only one black resident remained in Dunlap—eighty-four-year-old London Harness, who lived on the farm his grandparents purchased in 1879, the year of the exodus.

What happened to the blacks of Dunlap and other black settlements in Kansas? The majority moved to cities. In fact, among blacks, between 1870 and the beginning of the Great Depression, there was almost continuous movement from southern rural areas to the cities of the North. From that perspective, the post–Civil War migration to the West was an aberration, for it was a rural-to-rural movement.

Of all the movements of black people after Reconstruction ended, however, none was as spontaneous as that of the Exodusters. One of the most unusual episodes in the frontier movement, it removed significant numbers of blacks from the post–Civil War South and proved that many blacks were unwilling to accept economic and social victimization. Those blacks who were unwilling or unable to leave the South would remain in virtual bondage for another three quarters of a century. Southern blacks, however, would eventually live out the prophecy that Frederick Douglass set forth in the paper read in his absence at the American Social Science Association meeting in 1879. Through the civil rights movement of the 1950s and 1960s, the "authors of the prosperity, beauty and civilization of the South" did indeed become the "arbiters of her destiny."

Chronology

1776	Declaration of Independence issued; Revolutionary War begins
1777	Vermont is the first state to abolish slavery
1787	Constitutional Convention in Philadelphia provides for the return of escaped "persons owing service to another"
1790	First federal U.S. census shows approximately 757,000 blacks in the United States, out of a total population of 3,929,214; some 60,000 blacks were free
1793	First Fugitive Slave Act passed by Congress
1800	South Carolina prohibits free blacks from entering the state
1803	The Louisiana Purchase is made by the United States from France; Kansas is one of the territories included in that purchase
1804	Haiti becomes the second nation, and the first black nation, in the Western Hemisphere to secure its independence
1807	British Parliament abolishes the slave trade
1808	There are approximately one million enslaved African Americans in the United States; a federal ban on the importation of slaves takes effect as of January 1
c. 1809	Benjamin Singleton born
1816–1817	American Colonization Society founded
1821	Liberia founded on the west coast of Africa as a colony for free blacks from the United States
1822	First black settlers arrive in Liberia
1827	*Freedom's Journal*, the first black newspaper in the United States, begins publication in New York City; that same year, New York State abolishes slavery
1830s	The Underground Railroad has become well organized
c. 1833	Henry Adams born
1836	Free Frank McWorter founds New Philadelphia in Pike County, Illinois
1842	The Dawn Institute established in Dresden, Ontario, Canada, to teach fugitive slaves trades

1850	Fugitive Slave Act passed
	Edwin McCabe born
1854	Kansas-Nebraska Act empowers the people in individual territories to decide whether their territories will allow slavery
1859	Abolitionist John Brown leads an unsuccessful raid on the federal arsenal at Harper's Ferry, Virginia
1860	Republican Abraham Lincoln elected President of the United States
	There are 625 free blacks and two slaves in the Kansas Territory
1861	Seven southern states secede from the Union and form the Confederate States of America; four more southern states soon join the Confederacy
	Confederates fire on federal Fort Sumter in Charleston Harbor, and the Civil War begins
1862	Congress authorizes the Union Pacific and Central Pacific railroads to build a transcontinental line
	Congress passes the Homestead Act, enabling citizens or permanent immigrants to buy public land on the American frontier
1863	Lincoln's Emancipation Proclamation takes effect, freeing all slaves in the Confederate states
1864	Union General William Tecumseh Sherman undertakes his "march to the sea," aimed at cutting the Confederacy in half
1865	Bureau of Freedmen, Refugees, and Abandoned Lands created by Congress
	Abraham Lincoln assassinated; Vice President Andrew Johnson succeeds to the presidency
	Congress approves the Thirteenth Amendment to the U.S. Constitution, abolishing slavery
	Presidential Reconstruction begins
	Southern Reconstruction legislators pass rigid labor-control laws called Black Codes
1866	Ku Klux Klan founded in Pulaskie, Tennessee
1869	Congress approves the Fourteenth Amendment to the U.S. Constitution, declaring that the right to vote cannot be denied because of race, color, or previous condition of servitude
1870	Henry Adams and other blacks in Louisiana form a committee to ascertain "the true condition of our race"
	The black population of Kansas numbers 17,108
1871	Congress passes the Ku Klux Klan Act, declaring certain crimes against individuals as violations of federal law
1872	Congress forms a Joint Select Committee to Inquire into the Condition of Affairs in the Late Insurrectionary States and begins to hold hearings
1873	Panic of 1873 ushers in a severe nationwide depression
	Benjamin Singleton visits Kansas to inquire about colonization
1874	Edwin McCabe heads for Kansas
	Democrats take control of the U.S. House of Representatives

1875	Democrats retake control in Mississippi; their "Mississippi Plan" for readmission to the Union becomes a model for other former Confederate states
	Henry Adams's committee reforms itself as the Colonization Council
1876	America celebrates the centennial of its independence
	Singleton and others convene the first Emigration Convention, Nashville, Tennessee, May 19
	The presidential election is so close that in order for Republican Rutherford B. Hayes to assume the presidency, Republicans agree to withdraw all remaining federal troops from the South
1877	Federal troops withdrawn from the South, ending Reconstruction
	The Nicodemus Colony is plotted as government townsite in Graham County, Kansas
1878	Democrats regain control of southern states
	An epidemic of yellow fever ravages towns along the Mississippi River
1879	The Exodus of 1879
	The Colored People's Board of Emigration of the City of St. Louis incorporated
	Benjamin Singleton establishes the Singleton Colony in Morris County, Kansas
	The American Social Science Association takes up the question of the Exodusters at its annual meeting in September
1880	The black population of Kansas is 43,107
	A Senate Select Committee Investigating the "Negro Exodus from the Southern States" holds hearings; Henry Adams and Benjamin Singleton are among those who testify
1881	Benjamin Singleton forms the United Colored Links political party in Topeka, Kansas
1882	Edwin McCabe elected state auditor of Kansas; re-elected two years later
1883	Benjamin Singleton forms the Chief League to encourage black emigration to Cyprus
1884	Henry Adams last heard from, in Kansas
1889	The federal government opens up the Oklahoma Territory for settlement; Edwin McCabe soon establishes Langston City
1892	Benjamin Singleton dies in St. Louis, Missouri
1896	In *Plessy v. Ferguson*, the U.S. Supreme Court rules that "separate but equal" facilities are constitutional
1907	Oklahoma is admitted to statehood; its laws provide for legal segregation
1920	Edwin McCabe dies penniless in Chicago, Illinois

Bibliography

BOOKS

Athearn, Robert G. *In Search of Canaan: Black Migration to Kansas, 1879–1880*. Lawrence: Regents Press of Kansas, 1978.

Cutler, William G. *History of the State of Kansas*. Chicago: A.T. Andreas, 1883.

Dann, Martin E., ed. *The Black Press, 1827–1890*. New York: Capricorn Books, 1971.

Douglass, Frederick. *Life and times of Frederick Douglass: Written by Himself*. Reprint, New York: Collier Books, 1962.

Foner, Eric. *Reconstruction: America's Unfinished Revolution, 1863–1877*. New York: Harper & Row, 1988.

Greenberg, Jonathan. *Staking a Claim: Jake Simmons, Jr., and the Making of an African-American Oil Dynasty*. New York: Macmillan Publishing Co., 1990.

Kaplan, Sidney. *The Black Presence in the Era of the American Revolution, 1770-1800*. New York: New York Graphic Society, Ltd., 1973.

Katz, William Loren. *The Black West: A Documentary and Pictorial History*. Revised ed. New York: Doubleday & Co., Inc., 1973.

Levine, Bruce, et al. *Who Built America?* Vol. 1: *From Conquest and Colonization Through Great Reconstruction and the Great Uprising of 1877*. New York: Pantheon Books, 1989.

McFeely, William S. *Frederick Douglass*. New York: W. W. Norton, Inc., 1991.

Martin, Waldo E., Jr. *The Mind of Frederick Douglass*. Chapel Hill: University of North Carolina Press, 1984.

Painter, Nell Irvin. *Exodusters: Black Migration to Kansas After Reconstruction*. New York: W. W. Norton, 1986.

Sterling, Dorothy, ed. *The Trouble They Seen: Black People Tell the Story of Reconstruction*. New York: Doubleday & Co., Inc., 1976.

Walker, Juliet E. K. *Free Frank: A Black Pioneer on the Antebellum Frontier*. Lexington: University Press of Kentucky, 1983.

BOOKS FOR CHILDREN

Adams, Russell L. *Great Negroes Past and Present*. Chicago: Afro-Am Publishing Co., 1984.

Bair, Barbara. *Though Justice Sleeps: African Americans 1880–1900*. New York: Oxford University Press, 1997.

130

Brenner, Barbara. *Wagon Wheels*. New York: HarperCollins, 1993.

Burt, Olive W. *Negroes in the Early West*. New York: Julian Messner, 1969.

Haskins, Jim. *Black, Blue & Gray: African Americans in the Civil War*. New York: Simon & Schuster, 1998.

————. *Get on Board: The Story of the Underground Railroad*. New York: Scholastic, Inc., 1993.

Heard, J. Norman. *The Black Frontiersmen: Adventures of Negroes Among American Indians 1528–1918*. New York: The John Day Company, 1969.

Katz, William Loren. *Black Legacy: A History of New York's African Americans*. New York: Atheneum, 1997.

ARTICLES

Entz, Gary R. "Image and Reality on the Kansas Prairie: 'Pap' Singleton's Cherokee County Colony." *Kansas History* 19 (Summer 1996): 124–139.

Hickey, Joseph V. "'Pap' Singleton's Dunlap Colony: Relief Agencies and the Failure of a Black Settlement in Eastern Kansas." *Great Plains Quarterly* 11 (Winter 1991): 23–36.

Peoples, Morgan D. "Kansas Fever in North Louisiana." *Louisiana History* 11 (Spring 1970): 121–135.

Schwendemann, Glen. "Nicodemus: Negro Haven on the Solomon," *Kansas Historical Quarterly* vol. XXXIV, no. 1 (Spring 1968): 10–31.

Strickland, Arvarh E. "Toward the Promised Land: The Exodus to Kansas and Afterward," *Missouri Historical Review* 69 (July 1975): 376-412.

"The Exodusters on the Missouri," *Kansas Historical Quarterly* vol. XXIX, no. 1 (Spring 1963): 25–40.

"The Negro Exodus from the Gulf States," *Journal of Science* 11 (May 1880).

"Wyandotte and the First 'Exodusters' of 1879," *Kansas Historical Quarterly* vol. XXVI, no. 3 (Autumn 1960): 233–49.

INTERNET SOURCES

The West Film Project, WETA, developed by Lifetime Learning Systems, 1996. http://www.pbs.org/weta/the west

GOVERNMENT RECORDS

Senate Report 693, 46th Congress, 2nd Session.

Source Notes

1. Dorothy Sterling, ed., *The Trouble They Seen: Black People Tell the Story of Reconstruction.* (New York: Doubleday & Co., Inc., 1976), pp. 6-8.
2. Ibid.
3. Ibid.
4. "Testimony of Benjamin Singleton, Washington, D.C., April 17,1880, before the Senate Select Committee Investigating the 'Negro Exodus from the Southern States.'" The West Film Project, WETA, developed by Lifetime Learning Systems, 1996. http://www.pbs.org/weta/the west/
5. Sterling, pp. 270-274.
6. Ibid., p. 271.
7. Senate Report 693, 46th Congress, 2nd Session, pp. 190-191.
8. Sterling, p. 77.
9. Nell Irvin Painter, *Exodusters: Black Migration to Kansas After Reconstruction.* (New York: W. W. Norton, 1986), p. 78.
10. Ibid., p. 80.
11. Bruce Levine et al, *Who Built America?* Vol. I: *From Conquest and Colonization Through Great Reconstruction and the Great Uprising of 1877.* (New York: Pantheon Books, 1989), p. 400.
12. Ibid., p. 513.
13. Martin E. Dann, editor, *The Black Press, 1827-1890.* (New York: Capricorn Books, 1971), p. 268.
14. Sidney Kaplan, *The Black Presence in the Era of the American Revolution, 1770-1800.* (New York: New York Graphic Society, Ltd., 1973), pp. 138-140.
15. Sterling, p. 58
16. Gary R. Entz, "Image and Reality on the Kansas Prairie: 'Pap' Singleton's Cherokee County Colony." *Kansas History* 19 (Summer 1996), p. 127
17. Levine et al, p. 400.
18. William Loren Katz, *The Black West: A Documentary and Pictorial History.* Revised ed. (New York: Doubleday & Co., Inc., 1973), p. 108.
19. Ibid., p. 168.
20. Levine et al, p. 513.
21. Entz, p. 133.
22. Ibid., p. 135.

23. Ibid., p. 133.
24. Ibid, p. 132.
25. Ibid, p. 134.
26. Dann, p. 269.
27. Robert G. Athearn, *In Search of Canaan: Black Migration to Kansas, 1879-80.* (Lawrence: Regents Press of Kansas, 1978), p. 80.
28. Painter, p. 198.
29. Ibid., p. 225.
30. Athearn, p. 37.
31. Ibid., p. 39.
32. Ibid., pp. 39-40.
33. Joseph V. Hickey, "'Pap' Singleton's Dunlap Colony: Relief Agencies and the Failure of a Black Settlement in Eastern Kansas." *Great Plains Quarterly* 11 (Winter 1991), p. 27.
34. Ibid.
35. Athearn, p. 78.
36. Katz, p. 256.
37. Painter, p. 237.
38. Ibid.
39. Frederick Douglass, *Life and Times of Frederick Douglass: Written By Himself.* (Reprint, New York: Collier Books, 1962), p. 248.
40. William S. McFeely, *Frederick Douglass.* (New York: W. W. Norton, Inc., 1991), p. 301.
41. "The Negro Exodus from the Gulf States," Journal of Science 11 (May 1880), pp. 1-2.
42. Waldo E. Martin, Jr. *The Mind of Frederick Douglass.* (Chapel Hill: University of North Carolina Press, 1984), p. 75.
43. Sterling, pp. 437-438.
44 Ibid., p. 479.
45. Testimony of Benjamin Singleton, Washington, D.C., April 17, 1880.
46. Ibid.
47. Ibid.
48. Painter, p. 252.
49. Ibid., p. 254.
50. Jonathan Greenberg, *Staking a Claim: Jake Simmons, Jr., and the Making of an African-American Oil Dynasty.* (New York: Macmillan Publishing Co., 1990), p. 60.
51. Barbara Bair. *Though Justice Sleeps: African Americans 1880-1900.* (New York: Oxford University Press, 1997), p. 21.
52. Hickey, p. 23.

Index

Page numbers in *italics* refer to illustrations

Adams, Henry
    colonization efforts of, 57–58, 60
    the Committee and, 42, 45
    grand jury service of, 46
    Kansas and, 76, 78
    local politics and, 45
    Reconstruction government and, 40
    testimony before Senate Committee on
        the Negro Exodus, 115–116, 121
    treatment by whites, 32, 34–36
    as undercover agent, 46
Allain, T.T., 111
American Colonization Society (ACS), 58,
    60, 124, 125
American Social Science Association, 112,
    126
Anthony, George T., 85
Atchison, Andrew, 103

Black Codes, 36, 39, 52, 115
black suffrage, 32, 39, 40, *41*, 45, 52, 78,
    115–116
Blair, Henry, 118
Border Ruffians, 67, 68
Brown, John, 68
Brown, Randall, 81
Bureau of Freedmen, Refugees, and
    Abandoned Lands (see Freedmen's
    Bureau)

Canaan, 14
Canada, 22

Cape Mesurado, 58
Carter, Henry, 81
cattle ranching, 69, 125
Chief League, 122
Chinese immigrants, 115
Civil Rights Bill of 1867, 39–40
Civil War, 14, 22–23, 25, *26*, 27, 31–32, 69
Clay, Henry, 22
colonization, 57, 58, *59*, 60
Colonization Council, 57–58, 60
Colored People's Cooperative Emigration
    Club, 82
Committee, the, 42, 45
Confederate States of America, 22–23, 25,
    27, 31, 35, 39
congressional elections
    of 1874, 50
    of 1876, 60
    of 1878, 76, 78
Constitution of the United States, 20
    Fifteenth Amendment, 40
    Fourteenth Amendment, 40, 52
    Thirteenth Amendment, 35, 39, 52
Contrabands, 26
Conway, Thomas H., 96
Cyprus, 122

Davidson County, Nashville, Tennessee, 19
Davis, Jefferson, 25
Dawn Institute, Dresden, Ontario, 22
DeFrantz, Alonzo, 86
Democratic Party, 50, 52, 60, 76
depression, 49–50
Douglas, Stephen A., 66

Douglass, Frederick, 52, *53*, 54, 68, 89, 111–113, 126
dugouts, 75
Dunlap, Joseph, 86
Dunlap Colony, Morris County, Kansas, 85–86, 103, 125, 126

Edgefield Real Estate Association, 81, 83
education, 32, 103, *123*, 126
Emancipation Proclamation, 23, *24*, 25, 31, *33*, *37*, 52
Emigrant Aid Association, 100, 112
Enforcement Acts, 40, 41
Exodus, Book of, 14–15, 54
Exoduster movement, 14, 16, 91, *92-93*, 94, *95*, 96, 99–100, *101*, 102–103, *104-105*, 106–108, 111–113, *114*, 115–118, 126

Field Order Number 15, 27
Fifteenth Amendment to the Constitution, 40
Fletcher, Jenny Smith, 74
Fletcher, Z.T., 74
Fort Sumter, 22
Fourteenth Amendment to the Constitution, 40, 52
Freedmen's Academy of Kansas, 103, 126
Freedmen's Aid Association, 103
Freedmen's Bureau, 32, *33*, 39
free-soilers, 68
Fugitive Slave Law of 1850, 20, 22
fugitive slaves, 20, *21*, 22

Garfield, James A., 115
German immigrants, 113, 115
Grant, Ulysses S., 42, 46, 50
Great Depression, 126
Green, Lafayette, 107
Greenbacks, 122
Greener, Richard T., 112–113

Hambleton, W.C., 45
Hamilton County, Indiana, 64
Harness, London, 126
Harper's Ferry, Virginia, 68
Hayes, Rutherford B., 52, 60
Hill, W.R., 69
Homestead Act of 1862, 65–66, 85
Hughes, Langston, 122

Ingalls, John J., 115

Israelites, 14, *15*

Jay Cooke and Company, 49
Jennings, Thomas L., 58, 60
Johnson, Andrew, 32, 35, 39
Johnson, Columbus M., 83
Joint Select Committee to Inquire into the Condition of Affairs in the Late Insurrectionary States, 45

Kansa Indians, 86
Kansas, 64, 66, *67*, 68–69, *70-71*, 72–76, 78, 82–83, *84*, 85, 86, 90–91, 96, 100, 125–126
Kansas City, Kansas, 102
Kansas Freedmen's Relief Association (KFRA), 103, 106
Kansas-Nebraska Bill of 1854, 66, 68
Keith, George, 103
Kellogg, William Pitt, 46
Kinsley Colony, Hodgeman County, Kansas, 106–107
Knowles, Robert, 81
Ku Klux Klan, 40, *41*, *43*
Ku Klux Klan Act of 1871, 40

labor contracts, 34, 36
Langston, John Mercer, 122
Langston City, Oklahoma, 122
Liberia, 58, 60, 124
Liberian Exodus Joint-Stock Steamship Company, 124
Lincoln, Abraham, 22, 23, 25, 27, 31–32
literacy requirements, 52
Louisiana Purchase, 66

manumission settlements, 64
McCabe, Edwin P., 76, *77*, 108, 121, 122, 124
McCabe Town Company, 122
McWorter, Frank, 64
Meridien, Mississippi, 40
Mississippi Plan, 50
Mississippi River, *95*, 96
Montgomery, Isaiah, 106
Moses, 14
Muldie family, 75, 76
My Larger Education (Washington), 124

Napier, H.A., 82
Nast, Thomas, *37*

136

National Colored Colonization Society, 60
Native American Indians, 64, 65, 75, 86
New England Emigrant Aid Society, 68
New Philadelphia, 64–65
New York African Society for Mutual Relief, 58
New York Stock Exchange, 49
Nicodemus Colony, Graham County, Kansas, 69, *70-71, 72–75*

Oklahoma territory, 122, *123*, 124
Osage Indians, 75
Osborn, Thomas A., 82
Overstolz, Henry, 100

Panic of 1873, 49
Pierce, Franklin, 66
Pinchback, P.B.S., 111
Polk, Elias, 81
poll taxes, 52
presidential election of 1876, 52, 60
Presidential Reconstruction, 35–36, 39
Proclamation of Amnesty and Reconstruction, 31
Promontory Pike, Utah, 65
Pulaskie, Tennessee, 40

Radical Reconstruction, 39–42, 45, 50, 52
railroads, 65, 69, 115
Reconstruction, 27, 89
    Presidential, 35–36, 39
    Radical, 39–42, 45, 50, 52
Reconstruction Act of 1867, 39
redemption, 52
Reeder, Andrew H., 68
repatriation, 58, 122, 124–125
Republican Party, 50, 52, 60, 68, 76, 78, 108
Roberts Settlement, Hamilton County, Indiana, 64
Roundtree, S.P., 72

St. Louis, Missouri, 94, 99–100, *101*
Salisbury family, *114*
Sea Islands, 31
Senate Select Committee on the Negro Exodus, 115–118, 121
sharecroppers, 113
Sherman, William Tecumseh, 25, 27
Singleton, Benjamin "Pap," 31, 36, *38*, 39, 63, 103, 115, 121

Singleton, Benjamin "Pap," (*continued*)
    birth of, 19
    in Civil War, 23
    escape from slavery, 20
    Kansas and, 64, 81–83, 85, 86, 90
    political activities of, 121–122
    testimony before Senate Committee on the Negro Exodus, 116–118
Singleton Colony, Cherokee County, Kansas, 83, *84*, 85
Sizemore, W.A., 82, 86
slavery, 13, 14, *15*, 27, 66
    fugitive slaves, 20, *21*, 22
    Thirteenth Amendment abolishes, 35
    Underground Railroad and, 20
Smith, W.H., 74
Snodgrass, John M., 103
soddies, 75
Stanton, Edwin, 27
state's rights, 20, 22

Tandy, Charleton H., 99, 100
Thirteenth Amendment to the Constitution, 35, 39, 52
Tilden, Samuel J., 52
Topeka, Kansas, 103, *104-105*
Trans-Atlantic Society, 122
Truth, Sojourner, 111
Turner, Henry McNeal, 124
Turner, J. Milton, 111

Underground Railroad, 20, 106
unemployment, 50
Union Army, 25
United Colored Links, 121–122

voting rights, 32, 39, 40, *41*, 45, 52, 78, 115–116

Wabaunsee Colony, Wabaunsee County, Kansas, 106
Wadkins, Daniel, 81
wagon trains, 65
War of Independence, 19
Washington, Booker T., 124
Watson, Maggie, 103
White League, *43*, 45, 46
white supremacy, 40
Windom, William, 118
Wyandotte, Kansas, 102

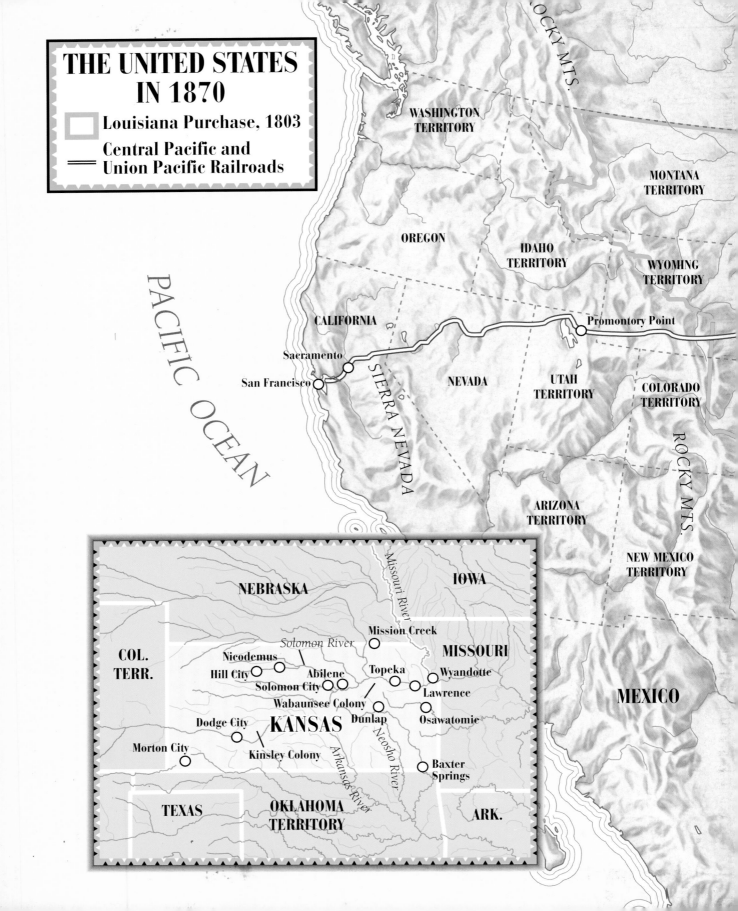

THE UNITED STATES IN 1870

Louisiana Purchase, 1803

Central Pacific and
Union Pacific Railroads

WASHINGTON TERRITORY

OREGON

IDAHO TERRITORY

MONTANA TERRITORY

WYOMING TERRITORY

CALIFORNIA

Promontory Point

PACIFIC OCEAN

Sacramento

San Francisco

SIERRA NEVADA

NEVADA

UTAH TERRITORY

COLORADO TERRITORY

ROCKY MTS.

ARIZONA TERRITORY

NEW MEXICO TERRITORY

MEXICO

ROCKY MTS.

NEBRASKA

IOWA

COL. TERR.

Solomon River

Missouri River

Mission Creek

MISSOURI

Nicodemus

Hill City

Abilene

Topeka

Wyandotte

Solomon City

Lawrence

Wabaunsee Colony

Dodge City

Dunlap

Osawatomie

Morton City

Kinsley Colony

KANSAS

Arkansas River

Neosho River

Baxter Springs

TEXAS

OKLAHOMA TERRITORY

ARK.